Achieving Success with Your Leadership Project

Education at SAGE

SAGE is a leading international publisher of journals, books, and electronic media for academic, educational, and professional markets.

Our education publishing includes:

- accessible and comprehensive texts for aspiring education professionals and practitioners looking to further their careers through continuing professional development

- inspirational advice and guidance for the classroom

- authoritative state of the art reference from the leading authors in the field

Find out more at: **www.sagepub.co.uk/education**

Achieving Success with Your Leadership Project

David Middlewood & Ian Abbott

Los Angeles | London | New Delhi
Singapore | Washington DC

SAGE Publications Ltd
1 Oliver's Yard
55 City Road
London EC1Y 1SP

SAGE Publications Inc.
2455 Teller Road
Thousand Oaks, California 91320

SAGE Publications India Pvt Ltd
B 1/I 1 Mohan Cooperative Industrial Area
Mathura Road
New Delhi 110 044

SAGE Publications Asia-Pacific Pte Ltd
33 Pekin Street #02-01
Far East Square
Singapore 048763

Library of Congress Control Number: 2011921274

British Library Cataloguing in Publication data

A catalogue record for this book is available from the British Library

ISBN 978-0-85702-366-7
ISBN 978-0-85702-367-4 (pbk)

Typeset by C&M Digitals (P) Ltd, Chennai, India
Printed in India at Replika Press Pvt Ltd
Printed on paper from sustainable resources

Contents

About the Authors

David Middlewood is a part-time Research Fellow at The University of Warwick, UK, having previously worked for the Universities of Leicester and Lincoln. At Leicester he was Deputy Director of the Centre for Educational Leadership and Management, and Director of school-based Masters Level programmes. He had a successful career in schools before entering Higher Education (HE), including nine years as headteacher of a secondary school.

David has taught and researched in various countries and been a visiting professor in New Zealand and South Africa. He has published over a dozen books, including several on Human Resource Management (HRM) topics (with Tony Bush) and ones on practitioner research, strategic management, curriculum management, creating a learning school and on extended schools. He was series editor for Sage's 'Leadership for Social Justice' series and was co-editor of two practitioner journals in the UK from 1999 to 2006. His research projects have included ones on support staff, programmes for new leaders, successful leadership teams, leadership and diversity in Further Education, and inclusiveness in schools. He also supports student research as a researcher in residence at a group of Leading Edge schools.

Ian Abbott is an associate professor at the University of Warwick, UK. He was formerly the deputy director of the Institute of Education at the university. He has led a number of programmes there including the MA in Educational Studies and the MA in Business and Enterprise and he has been Director of Teacher Education. He is currently the national co-ordinator at Warwick for the Teach First programme and he is Director of External Relations for the Institute of Education. Prior to joining the university he had a successful career in schools and colleges, including being Head of a Business Studies Department in a secondary school.

Ian has taught in a number of countries and has been involved in a wide range of major research projects. He has been editor of the journal of the Economics and Business Education Association. He has published a large number of journal articles and books, including a number on Teacher

Education. His research projects have included ones on the establishment and development of leadership teams, creative governance in Further Education and school funding.

David and Ian have worked, taught and tutored together in the UK and other countries on various leadership and management programmes at Masters Level.

Preface

The origins of this book lie in a number of informal conversations between the authors, especially during breaks between teaching sessions in a country where the temperatures and the humidity are consistently high. We found ourselves constantly aware of the large number of students studying at Masters Level in Leadership and/or Management – and a certain number of tutors also – who had expressed concern that there was no single text to which reference might be made for practical, straightforward information and guidance about their work, especially their final projects or dissertations. Further, more systematic enquiries later confirmed this need, and the general idea for such a text developed into this book.

One of the reasons for writing a book such as this is that the majority of the students concerned are part-time, fitting their study into the hours outside their main work as full-time professional practitioners. This leaves these teachers, lecturers, nurses, social workers, accountants, administrative staff, housing officers, retail management trainees and others with too little time to consult some of the detailed texts which the professional researcher is able to access. We have made reference to a number of such texts, especially in our 'Further Reading' at the end of chapters, and those readers who are drawn into the complexities of more advanced data analysis or methodological approaches, for example, should refer to such texts to supplement our guidance here. Many students are 'sponsored' by employers for part or all of their work, but many are completely self-funding and in all cases are under great pressures of time to successfully complete the programme and the final project report. Sometimes, career advancement can depend on such success.

The book is intended for those studying at Masters Level in an area with a component of leadership or management involved, in such areas as education, business studies or social studies. With the need for Masters Level qualifications increasing all the time (for example, at Postgraduate Certificate in Education (PGCE)), we believe the book will provide an invaluable resource for all such people. It is rooted both in our own experience of teaching, tutoring and supporting many students on a range of programmes in various countries, and in the experiences of those students themselves. This is why we have included a number of Case Examples to illustrate from students' actual experiences the realities of work at this level. (No students' or organisations' real names are used in these.) All the examples of pro-formas used in the book are adapted from ones used at the Institute of Education of the University of Warwick, but they are typical of those used at most Higher Education (HE) institutions in the United Kingdom.

Whether you are aiming to produce a final piece of work which is called a 'dissertation' or a 'project', the format of the book is intended to be easily accessible to all readers, with chapter introductions, summaries and the stressing of particularly important points. We examine all those issues raised with us by students, namely:

- What research is and how to decide on your topic
- Designing the research
- How to write a literature review
- How to decide on your methodology and then apply it
- Particular issues involved in research as a practitioner
- How to present and analyse your data
- How to write up the final report
- Making the most of the support available
- Understanding how your work is assessed.

Practical issues such as how to structure your project and how to reference your work are all included because in some cases the difference between success or failure can depend on very small points. We wish to stress, however, that all readers need to ensure they are aware of the precise requirements of the particular HE institution to which they are submitting their work, as regulations do vary and it is impossible for us to include all such variations in one text. Therefore, please make sure you carefully read the guidance that you are provided with by your particular HE institution. Similarly, this book in no way attempts to replace your most valuable support – your tutor. He or she remains one of the keys to your success and we hope the book will be helpful to tutors as well.

We would like to thank various people for their invaluable support, especially Kanta Chauhan for her excellent skills in making our work into a coherent whole, those at Sage Publications, especially Marianne Lagrange, and Tony Bush for his statistical assistance. Colleagues at the University of Warwick's Institute of Education and Business School have been helpful in giving feedback, and of course all the students past and present we have worked with have contributed considerably to the book's content and structure.

Finally, David thanks Jacqui and Ian thanks Deb for their personal support and tolerance in the writing of this book.

We wish everyone success in achieving their goal in Leadership and Management at Masters Level and hope that this book will help in some measure.

David Middlewood and Ian Abbott
January 2011

1

Setting the Scene

Introduction

Studying for a Masters Level qualification is a difficult, lengthy, but hopefully rewarding process. It should provide you with personal and professional satisfaction as you develop your own intellectual and professional capabilities. As you near the end of your programme of study you will be expected to complete a lengthy piece of work which is described in various ways in different institutions as a thesis, dissertation, extended study or project. During this book we will use the term 'project' to refer to any extended piece of Masters Level writing. The techniques we are writing about will be generally applicable to any extended Masters Level writing, but will be particularly focused on leadership and management. Carrying out a major project is the single most important aspect of Masters Level study and in this introductory chapter we will introduce and establish key ideas in this process.

In this chapter the following topics are considered:

- What is involved in completing your project?
- Are there special issues in leadership/management research?
- The nature of leadership and management
- How does your own role relate to the research context?

What is involved in completing your project?

As you start to consider your project you are likely to have already successfully completed a significant proportion of your Masters Level programme and be ready to undertake an intensive project over a number of months. You will already have written a number of assignments ranging from 1,000 to 5,000 words in length. In some of the assignments you will have carried out a literature review, reviewed policy documents, undertaken a case study; you may have collected and analysed data and you might even have conducted a small-scale research project. In many cases you will have received specific research methods training and written about particular methods of enquiry. You may also be thinking of developing an area that you have previously successfully written about. The skills you have already developed as part of your Masters Level programme will act as a useful starting point for the project. However, you will need to enhance your existing skills and to develop a range of additional skills to successfully complete your project.

So how does the project differ from your previous work? One immediate and obvious difference is the number of words required. The project can range from 10,000 to over 20,000 words depending on the requirements of your institution. Even at the bottom end of the word scale it is likely to be a significant increase on anything you have written before. At first the prospect of having to write up to 20,000 words can appear daunting, especially if you have other commitments and have never done anything like this before. However, as you get into the detail of the project you are likely to find that the 20,000 word limit is too small to do justice to your chosen topic. At this preliminary stage that is probably difficult to believe, but you will hopefully soon discover just how easy it is to write up to 20,000 words, especially on a topic of personal interest. Of course those words have to be coherent, relevant and at the right level to meet the stringent Masters Level assessment criteria.

How do you get started on the project? An obvious starting point has to be your previous written work and you need to remember to build on the strengths you have already developed. The general requirements for working and writing at Masters Level will still apply and hopefully well developed habits will be continued and enhanced. You should be well aware of the assessment criteria for Masters Level and these will continue to provide a base for your work. The skills you have already acquired and the lessons learnt from completing previous written assignments will be equally applicable to writing your project. So you initially need to:

- Get yourself organised
- Be realistic about what you can achieve
- Identify an area that *you* would like to investigate
- Be aware of the specific requirements for the project
- Take advantage of the support and guidance that is available.

Getting yourself organised sounds obvious, but it is amazing how many students fail to heed this basic piece of advice. By getting yourself organised we mean adopting some fundamental principles to ensure that you are fully equipped to complete the project. Firstly, consider the time implications of undertaking this piece of work. You are likely to be doing your project over a concentrated period of time, usually between three months and a year, depending on whether you are a full- or part-time student. You need to clear time to enable you to carry out the necessary work, so look carefully at your commitments and make sure you set aside blocks of time. It is often easier to focus on the project for a concentrated period of time rather than having to constantly pick up work again. Secondly, making a plan will help you to make the most of your time. A clear programme and structure, including key milestones, for the duration of the project will help you to achieve an effective use of your time. Your milestones will include identifying dates to complete your literature review, carrying out the fieldwork, undertaking analysis and commencing writing up. However, it is important to remember that your plan should not be too rigid and it is acceptable, even desirable, to amend the plan to reflect changing circumstances as you proceed through your project. You will need to discuss your plan with your tutor and we consider this planning in Chapter Two.

Being realistic about what you can achieve relates to the time issues we have already identified, but it also applies to your choice of topic. We will return to this in more detail in the next chapter, but students tend to want to 'solve the problems of the world' in their project. While this is a laudable aim and hopefully reflects your enthusiasm and commitment to the area you have chosen to investigate, you've got to be realistic. You only have a limited amount of time and of course a restricted number of words for the project, so the topic has to be manageable. If you start with a topic that is too large you will soon run into trouble, so remember to be realistic about what you can achieve.

Choosing a topic to investigate that personally interests you will increase your motivation and make the process easier. This is a chance for you to conduct an in-depth investigation into a topic of great personal interest and you may never be given this opportunity again, so make sure you choose your topic carefully. However, there may be pressure from your line manager or those funding your Masters Level study to conduct an investigation that is deemed to be useful to your organisation. This is an understandable pressure given the constraints on funding and the desire to achieve value for money. You will have to balance these pressures, but remember that by studying for a Masters Level qualification you will benefit personally and this will in turn have a positive impact on your organisation. Ideally, you will be able to choose a topic that reflects your own interests, has a positive impact on your own practice and benefits the organisation more widely.

Your own HE institution will have specific guidance on what is required to successfully complete your Masters Level project. Make sure you are aware of these requirements and remember they may differ from those you have experienced when you completed your other assignments. They will be available either in printed form or electronically and it's worth spending some time checking on the detail. Higher Education institutions operate according to set procedures and routines, and no matter how ridiculous they may seem, these regulations have to be followed by all students, you will not be granted an exemption. Precious time and effort can be wasted by not following published guidelines. For example, marks can be deducted if word limit guidelines are not adhered to, and a completed project will not be marked if it does not conform to the presentation conventions. We will deal with such issues and look in detail at the assessment process in Chapter Ten.

There should be a wide range of support and guidance available for you to access as you navigate your way through your Masters Level project and we fully explore how to get the most from the available support in Chapter Eight. We have already said a little about the general documentary guidance available to you. For international students there is likely to be an international tutor who will be able to offer specialist support, especially in relation to access issues for research. You will also have a personal tutor who will be able to provide general support relating to non-project-specific issues, but the key person related to your Masters Level project will be your project supervisor or tutor. It is important that you establish a positive working relationship with your project supervisor or tutor who will either be an expert in your chosen area of study or in some aspect of research methodology. Having clear and consistent communication procedures are important and keeping in touch is vital. This is even more important when things are not going to plan. Your tutor will be able to act as a sounding board and to provide much needed reassurance as you progress through your period of study.

If you are a part-time student you will also be able to access support from your own institution, especially the leadership team who will be well placed to offer guidance on particular aspects of your research project. This might take the form of practical support in terms of providing information, access and most importantly time. Finally there are your fellow students who can provide an invaluable source of support and practical advice, and are especially aware of the particular pressures you are operating under.

Are there special issues in leadership/ management research?

So far, in this chapter, we have written about a range of general issues relating to your research project and explored how you actually get started. In the remainder of the chapter we are going to focus on more specific issues relating to leadership and management. Every subject area has particular issues and trends that reflect current concerns in the discipline. Over time these will change and new theories and approaches will emerge and become fashionable. Leadership and management is no different in this respect to any other subject area, and as a student of this area you will have spent a considerable amount of time looking at current theories and debates and how they have been developed and implemented. This should have enabled you to have built up a detailed knowledge and understanding of current issues within this area. Your research project should build on these issues and your knowledge and understanding to enable you to develop a deeper understanding of the theoretical and practical aspects of leadership and management. Your own research into leadership and management will provide you with opportunities to develop key ideas and concepts. We will continue to return to some of these during the book as we illustrate key issues in developing and carrying out your research project by giving practical examples based on current best practice.

Carrying out research into leadership and management will enable you to relate the theoretical aspects of your course to your own practice. This is likely to contribute to your own personal development and it may also lead to benefits for your present or future employer. Your research project is likely to involve looking at the implementation of particular theories. Research in leadership and management is much more likely to focus on the practical rather than the theoretical. Whilst there is a strong theoretical base to leadership and management, it is a living subject and is rooted in the improvement of the practice of individuals and organisations. Leadership and management theories are an essential part of developing your understanding of the area, but they also have to be applied in a practical context. In your research you are likely to have the opportunity to look at how theory actually works, in practice. In reality you may find that the application of theoretical concepts does not always lead to a positive outcome. A significant part of your research project could be finding out why desired outcomes have not been achieved and what lessons have been learnt. In many cases as much can often be learnt from research into one failed policy than into a number of successful initiatives. Students are often wary of looking at aspects of leadership and management that are not successful and want to focus on successful outcomes. Whilst this is an understandable response, you need to set this reticence aside and give yourself the best opportunity you can to develop a meaningful and worthwhile research project.

The nature of research into leadership and management often lends itself to the development of a case study approach. Basing your project in or around an organisation and a particular development is a tried and tested method for a Masters Level project. It may well be a method you have employed during other parts of your course and you can build on the lessons you have learnt earlier. Choosing a case study approach will enable you to develop a particular focus for your project and may provide you with a more manageable topic that is more appropriate to your particular needs. The tight focus for the project provided by a case study, will also enable you to investigate an area in greater depth and reduce the opportunities for 'project drift'. This does not mean that you can ignore the theoretical aspects of leadership and management or ignore the wider issues that might arise from your project, but a case study approach makes it easier to ensure that the focus of the project remains constant.

If you decide to adopt a case study approach a key factor will be the nature of the organisation and this will have an obvious impact on the structure and nature of your project. There are core issues in leadership and management, but different sectors will have different issues and priorities. If you are interested in the public sector and your case study is based around the health service or education, it is likely that the context will be different compared to students conducting research in the private sector in, for example, banking or manufacturing. However, it is important to remember that although the context might differ the principles remain the same. Concepts of the various aspects of leadership are still the same in education and the financial services sector. However, the context and the application of theories of leadership may well differ at any given time. Different approaches and models of leadership might be popular in individual organisations across different sectors at the same time. Each sector will have different priorities and what might be considered best practice in the health service might not be applicable for the retail sector. This does not stop policy makers attempting to import approaches from one sector into another. This might also be an issue you would want to investigate during your research project. At this stage you need to consider the possibility of developing a case study approach during your project, and we discuss in detail the strengths and weaknesses of adopting this type of research methodology in Chapter Two.

The nature of leadership and management

Effective leadership and management have been identified as important factors in the success of any organisation. Having successfully reached the project stage of your Masters Level programme you are probably fully acquainted with the debate surrounding the nature of leadership and management. You could be on a programme in leadership or management or both. The two terms, 'leadership' and 'management', are often used interchangeably. In many cases leadership is included as an aspect of management, but leading is not the same as managing.

At this stage in your Masters Level programme it is not very helpful that there are a number of definitions of leadership. Southworth (1993) describes leadership as a contested concept, and Yukl (2002: 4–5) claims that: 'there is a continuing controversy about the difference between leadership and management' and 'the definition of leadership is arbitrary and very subjective'. According to Bush, Bell and Middlewood (2010: 3) 'Leadership is independent of positional authority while management is linked directly to it'. Nahavandi (2000) goes further and argues that the two are distinctly different. A focus for these differences can be how leaders and managers deal with change. Cuban (1988: xx) illustrates this:

> By leadership, I mean influencing others' actions in achieving desirable ends. Leaders are people who shape the goals, motivations, and actions of others. Frequently they initiate change to reach existing and new goals. ... While managing well often exhibits leadership skills, the overall function is toward maintenance rather than change.

Nahavandi (2000: 13) argues that: 'Whereas leaders have long term and future-oriented perspectives and provide a vision for their followers that looks beyond their immediate surroundings, managers have short term perspectives and focus on routine issues within their own immediate departments or groups'.

For any organisation to operate effectively both leadership and management will have to be given sufficient emphasis. It is important to recognise the importance of change and new developments while maintaining effective operational efficiency. In any organisation there is a need for vision from leaders and also effective management towards clear goals.

If we accept that it is often difficult to define leadership and that there is a direct connection between leadership and management, how do you carry out research into this area? According to Burnes (2009: 492–3) researchers into leadership and management can be split into three groups:

- Those who primarily focus on the personal characteristics-traits of the leader
- Those who concentrate on the leader–follower situation, especially the characteristics of the follower
- Those who take a contextual approach by relating leadership and management styles to the overall organisation context and climate.

This provides a useful starting point as you begin to think about the focus of your research project. However, we would argue that this is a limited perspective and there are other dimensions you can consider when you carry out research in the broader field of leadership and management. These include:

- The leadership and management of particular policies and initiatives
- Dealing with change in the organisation
- Leadership and management of resources to ensure efficiency, effectiveness and equity
- Micro leadership of a particular environment or policies.

You will need to decide on a focus for your project and whilst there is clearly overlap between leadership and management it is likely that you will decide to concentrate on one particular area. It is important to remember that your project has to have a leadership and management focus, otherwise you will not be able to meet the criteria that have been identified. You cannot just focus on the policy or initiative you have decided to investigate – your project has to have a clear leadership and management focus. Sometimes students lose sight of that obvious fact because they get carried away with investigating their chosen topic.

The debate about the nature of leadership and management that we have considered in this section is something that you are likely to return to as you proceed through the research process. At this stage we have provided a brief introduction to the issues surrounding the different aspects of leadership and management and we now need to consider the part your own experience can play in developing your research project.

How does your own role relate to the research context?

Every student will bring their own experience and knowledge of leadership and management to their thinking about the focus for their research project. Most students will have some experience of being led and managed and many will also have been in a leadership or management position in an organisation. The project cannot be based solely on your own experience, but it can provide a useful starting point and provide a number of ideas that you might be able to develop. If you are currently working in an organisation and studying part-time or have been fortunate enough to get a secondment then you will be able to draw on your own work experience and organisation when considering research possibilities in leadership and management. You can start by examining your own role within your organisation to see if there are opportunities for research. You might be involved in a management or leadership role, or you might want to investigate aspects of these in the context of your employing or sponsoring organisation. A good starting point is to undertake a Strengths, Weaknesses, Opportunities and Threats (SWOT) analysis on your own role in relation to the opportunities for research. If we consider the case of a middle manager in a medium-sized organisation it might look something like the example shown in Figure 1.1.

Strengths	Weaknesses
Ease of access	Confidentiality
High level of expertise	Narrow area to investigate
Improve own practice	Confirmation of existing practice
Personal contacts	Limited perspective of findings
Opportunities	**Threats**
Consider new initiatives	Ethical issues
Investigate aspects of leadership	Having to follow the 'party line'
Raising your profile within the organisation	

Figure 1.1   SWOT analysis of your own role in relation to research opportunities

You will have to look at your own circumstances and weigh up the advantages and disadvantages, of conducting research in your own organisation. Drawing on your own experience and situation may help you to overcome some of the difficulties associated with carrying out research. For example, on a practical level access issues should be minimised and you should be able to utilise personal contacts to gather data. However, there are major ethical concerns, relating to confidentiality and potential conflict of interest associated with carrying out research into your own organisation. The major advantage from utilising your own role as the research context is that any findings will have a direct impact on your own performance. If you are carrying out research into leadership and management in the wider organisation, this will have an impact on the overall performance of the organisation. There could be a direct correlation between your research and your role within your organisation. However, you need to be aware that your findings may not be positive in terms of the organisation and you will need to carefully manage any feedback. There might be an expectation that your research supports existing practice within your organisation and this cannot be guaranteed.

You may decide to investigate aspects of your own practice or the wider organisation but you will have to make a number of decisions about the process. In particular:

- What is the context of the research?
- What aspects of leadership and management will you consider?
- Who are the leaders and managers?

Once you have identified a research topic deciding on the context of your research is an important first step. There is a 'golden rule' concerning the context of the research:

9

> Ensure the context is realistic and manageable before you embark on the project.

You may have the opportunity to focus on an existing issue in leadership and management in your organisation or to investigate a new policy initiative. These may relate directly to your own role, but you might want to take the role of an outsider and look at an area not directly related to your position within the organisation. This may limit the immediate personal benefits of the research, but will have wider implications for the organisation. You might want to look outside your own context and compare your organisation with what is happening elsewhere. The broader policy context might be another area you want to consider and again this might enable you to have an impact at a macro level. However, you have to be realistic and to acknowledge that in the vast majority of cases the outcomes from your project will have a restricted effect on the wider world, but nonetheless will, hopefully, have a valuable impact on your own practice and that of your organisation.

You will also need to identify what aspects of leadership and management you wish to look at. Earlier in the chapter we considered the differences between leadership and management. The first issue to determine is whether you are going to investigate leadership or management. In reality it is likely that you will look at aspects of both leadership and management, but you need to be clear about the distinction between the two areas. It may be that you want to look at a particular style of leadership or certain aspects of leadership such as the impact of leadership teams. In terms of management you may decide to look at aspects of management relating to a particular policy initiative or the ways in which effective utilisation of resources is maintained. Whatever your choice of topic, it is important to remember that the focus of your project has to be leadership and management.

Your taught course will have given you the opportunity to look in detail at leadership and management theory and practice. By the time you come to start your project you should be well versed in the different facets of leadership and management, across a diverse range of areas and ideas. For example, you will have considered issues associated with leading people and also looked at the management of financial resources. However, too often students come up with a wonderful idea for a project that is especially important to them in the context of their work, but closer scrutiny reveals that there is little or no connection to leadership and management. Obviously a significant part of the role of your tutor is to get you to focus in your project on leadership and management in theoretical *and* practical terms. Often this does not mean changing your chosen topic; instead you have to identify the aspects of leadership and management that are relevant for your topic.

So, in the initial thinking and planning of your project always remember to clearly relate your chosen area of investigation to aspects of leadership and management. Getting this right at an early stage will save time and effort later on in the process.

Finally there are some important decisions to be made regarding who are the leaders and managers in your area of investigation. Traditional hierarchical models of leadership and management lead us to believe relatively clear-cut distinctions can be made. The reality is often more problematic and in many organisations a confusing picture can often emerge. Models of distributed leadership provide opportunities for leadership to exist at a number of levels. For example, of particular interest for those working in an educational context is the idea of leadership in the classroom, while those operating in other sectors will also recognise there are many opportunities for leadership and management in different contexts across their organisation.

If you are a full-time student with little or no leadership or management experience you have to consider a number of other factors. You will face a set of different problems in identifying a suitable topic for your project. In particular you will not have immediate access to an organisation where you will be able to identify an area to investigate. You may not have the personal contacts to ensure access to an organisation. You will need to think carefully about your chosen area, your own knowledge and experience. The issues surrounding access are significant, and will have an important bearing on the structure and timing of your project, but they are not insurmountable. Your HE institution should have a support network in place to help you with problems of this nature. Your project tutor may well be the best person to help with problems of access. We will look in detail at how you can make the most of available support in Chapter Eight.

However, not being tied to a particular organisation does bring certain advantages and may allow you greater freedom to be more imaginative and critical. You will not have any pressure from an organisation to investigate a particular topic or to validate existing policies. You will not be limited in your choice of topic and can think more creatively and over a longer time period. You may also decide that the focus for your project is more likely to be on a macro rather than micro level. The opportunity to stand back and be truly independent may also enable you to provide a more critical commentary on particular initiatives and policy developments, unlike students who may be constrained by their employing, and in many cases funding, organisation.

In extreme cases your organisation will have directed you to investigate a particular area of concern. However, the reality for most students will be very different and you will be in a position to develop a project related to your own needs. Hopefully your course of study, experience and your own personal interests will have provided you with some ideas about the topic and direction for your project. In the next chapter we will provide specific guidance on how to identify a particular topic to investigate, design your research and the process you have to go through to get started on your research project.

 Summary of Chapter One

This chapter has:

- Provided an introduction to the context and structure of the research project in leadership and management
- Explored the nature of leadership and management as a focus for your research
- Identified special issues in leadership/management research and how these can be related to your particular situation
- Discussed how your own role within an organisation can relate to the research context.

 Further reading

Bush, T., Bell, L. and Middlewood, D. (2010) *Principles of Educational Leadership.* London: Sage.
Burnes, B. (2009) *Managing Change.* London: Prentice Hall.

2

Choosing your Topic and Designing the Research

Now that you are aware of what is involved in completing the Masters Level project in leadership and management, and considered your own situation as regards this, we are able to turn to more precise issues. This chapter therefore considers the following issues:

- What factors should be taken into account in selecting your personal topic
- The probable structure of your final project
- Submitting your proposal for approval
- Understanding the main research approaches and designing your research
- Being clear about case studies
- Reflecting upon the importance of the context and culture of research, especially in international work.

What factors should be considered in deciding upon your topic?

We can begin with a piece of advice – that we are confident all tutors, supervisors and advisers would agree with – that we propose as our second 'golden rule':

Choose a topic in which you have a genuine interest.

This seems very obvious but because of the many and various pressures upon them, a number of students, especially in the final stages of their programme, study a topic with which they become bored or tired. Up to 20,000 words is a great deal of writing on something which you felt you *ought* to study. It is demanding enough anyway, but if you are doing something that someone, however well meaning, pressured you into doing, you rarely perform at your best. As Chapter One suggested, completing this project should be developing your intellectual and professional capabilities and this development will not happen if you begin to 'switch off' during the research. Even with the most fascinating topic, there will still be a few periods during completion when you see some of the work as a chore anyway. If the whole project becomes a chore, it will be a piece of work well below what might have been achieved and the whole period of study will not be enjoyable.

It is sometimes suggested that your choice of topic can be aided if you consider what interests you most under a list of headings such as people, places, events, concepts. Some students are drawn to concepts of, for example, equality, relationships, mentoring, authority, motivation, and so on. Others are intrigued by places such as staffrooms, residential homes, school playgrounds, staff cafeteria, whilst some students have been stimulated by events such as staff social occasions, company mergers, conferences, or even local political elections. Many begin with an interest in a particular group of people such as disabled staff or pupils, ethnic minority managers, inductees or pre-retirement staff. Again, anything which confirms your interest is helpful.

Your personal topic which you decide on therefore should, ideally:

- Be of personal interest to you
- Be relevant to your professional life and career, now and in the future
- Give you the opportunity to develop new knowledge, skills and understanding
- Be challenging, but within your own capabilities.

Use this as a checklist when you have chosen your topic. You should be able to tick at least three of the four if you have got the right topic.

We now need to examine some of the practical factors which you may wish to consider in selecting your topic.

Should I research a fresh topic or one studied in a previous assignment?

This is the most commonly asked question by Masters Level students when trying to decide on a project or dissertation topic. As always, there is no simple answer to suit everyone. See Figure 2.1 for a simple summary of some arguments for and against choosing a new or familiar topic.

As you can see, the issues relate to avoiding the boredom mentioned above and considering the practicalities of reading, saving time and so on. We suggest

Fresh Topic	Familiar Topic
• You will not be 'stale' and can look at the topic with fresh eyes	• You have done a good deal of the reading already
• You need to find new respondents – your previous field is 'used up'	• You will save time
• The topic was not a prominent one when you did previous work	• You can use previous work as a starting point
• The topic represents a new interest for you	• Your 'contacts' are well established

Figure 2.1   Arguments for a fresh or familiar topic

that, prior to discussion with your tutor and submitting your proposal, you look back at your previous assignments submitted and assessed during the programme. Try to answer these questions:

- Which one(s) did you enjoy the most?
- Which one(s) got the best grade?
- Were there any where you wished you had had more words available?
- Did you feel in any that you had only scratched the surface of what you were researching and wished you could have explored further?
- Did the feedback you received on any of them suggest further study would be or would have been helpful?
- Was there one where you felt you received particularly helpful and expert guidance which could be available again for your project?

You also need to consider the amount of literature available on any topic. Is the topic 'well worn' or relatively under-researched? The next chapter deals fully with all such literature issues in considering your literature review, but it may help you at this stage to think about your own attitude. Is seeking the literature an exciting part for you? Do you get frustrated if you cannot seem to access sufficient reading?

Some students believe strongly that choosing a familiar topic is better because the fact that some of the reading has probably been done will save them lots of valuable time. Whilst this is true, it will not compensate for the fact that you might become bored with the actual reading on that topic, as mentioned above.

However, considering the time available for your project completion is undoubtedly a factor you might consider in deciding on a topic. How much time can you realistically set aside for the work? You will have a final submission date agreed with your institution via your tutor. Work back from that and be aware of particular blocks of time in your personal, domestic and professional calendar. For example, Christmas is a notoriously difficult time in many countries in which to get much work done, even though educational and business institutions are mostly closed for up to two weeks. Ramadan can be a difficult period for some students when a very restricted diet leaves many of them needing more sleep and also sometimes feeling 'light-headed'. Other times will be very personal to the individual student, such as an impending family birth or special anniversary – no qualification is worth risking family relationships for!

In addition, you may know that you are taking on a new work role during the next few months, even changing institutions. These are demanding times and should be allowed for if possible in your planned schedule.

Finally, there will be the unexpected – of course. Plan for the unexpected by allowing some 'slack' time in your schedule and be prepared to adjust accordingly!

Having decided on the broad topic you wish to research, you now need to be clear about the precise purpose and focus of your research. A clear statement of purpose is essential for your project, otherwise your research risks being unfocused. As mentioned in Chapter One, many students can be initially over-ambitious in their choice of topic. Let us consider a topic that we have seen students in both the private and public sectors express interest in, usually because of personal experience – the merger of two or more institutions. These could be schools, colleges, local businesses, medical centres, and so on. If this is the broad topic, consider these potential titles:

(a) 'To examine the impact of the merger of two schools, businesses or organisations'
(b) 'To discover whether staff catering facilities were adequate for the combined staff'
(c) 'To investigate whether the separate IT systems were compatible'
(d) 'To discover whether "demoted" staff still felt loyalty to the organisation'.

Each of this has obvious serious defects:

(a) is far too broad
(b) is too trivial
(c) is too technical, and
(d) risks being unethical.

None of them has in any case a specific leadership focus. Ask yourself what really interests you about the merger:

- The human relationships and which group(s) in particular?
- The management structure and/or culture?

- The efficient use of resources?
- The productivity of the new organisation (its effectiveness)?
- The actual merger process (examining the change management)?
- Value for money?

(or others?)

Then you can begin to focus down on a potential title. You may also wish to clarify what it is you are trying to achieve through the research. Are you trying, for example, to:

- Evaluate?
- Explain how or why something happened?
- Describe a process?

(Denscombe, 2002: 28)

Or perhaps you feel strongly that a particular group of people were ignored or treated badly during the merger and you wish to investigate their situation and apply objectivity to this.

When you have settled on a topic, it can be a useful exercise to do a simple list of resources you will need before submitting your proposal, which is dealt with in a later section of this chapter. Have you checked that you have or will have:

- Sufficient time (the most important resource and already discussed)?
- Sufficient finance (for example, for postage, travel, computer accessories, possible purchase of books)?
- Access to a library (check your library card does not expire halfway through the project!)?
- Permission from relevant authorities to proceed?
- Support from, for example, family, colleagues etc.?

Although it is a secondary consideration, your chosen topic, whatever it is, should give you the opportunity to develop specific skills, as mentioned in Chapter One. These are likely to be of considerable use to you in your later career. Jankowicz (2004) suggests that these may include:

- Interviewing
- Negotiating and persuading
- Organising, including managing your time
- Analytical skills
- Summarising
- Acceptance of 'grey areas' in conclusions
- Report writing.

Likely structure of a final project or dissertation

It is vital that you read carefully and understand the precise requirements of the HE institution which is to be assessing your project. The requirements are likely to give an indication of the relative importance (through a number of words or marks allocated) of different sections of the final piece of work. It is important therefore that you conform to these requirements which may differ somewhat from institution to institution. (For detailed guidance on assessment procedures, see Chapter Ten.) However, at Masters Level, there are sufficient commonalities across HE for us to be able to suggest that the structure of your work should include the following:

- An introductory section – probably stating something about the topic in broad terms, about the writer and reason for or links with the topic
- Context section – describing the professional context within which the project takes place
  (The above sections may be required to be combined into one.)
- Purpose – a clear statement about the overall purpose of the project is essential. This is likely to be linked with some specific research aims and probably the specific research questions.

As an example of the last point, Heather's research statement was: 'The purpose of this project therefore is to investigate the impact of the merger of two local businesses on the daily working practices of middle managers.'

Her research aims were:

- To discover the extent to which practices had changed
- To ascertain whether the managers preferred the new ones or not
- To investigate the reasons for liking or disliking these practices
- To evaluate the overall impact on the managers' morale.

These aims would eventually be turned into specific research questions.

- A Literature Review section (see Chapter Three)
- A Research Methodology section (see Chapter Four)
- A section presenting the findings of your research (see Chapter Seven)
- Analysis section (see Chapter Seven)
- Conclusions and recommendations section (see Chapter Seven).

In addition, you will need to supply an abstract, separate from the main body of the work, any appendices, and a bibliography (see Chapter Nine for details of all these). Note that the abstract can only be done at the conclusion of your work.

We remind you that any of the above may be combined in various ways, according to specific requirements, so please ensure you check these carefully as they apply to your own institution. Because of these variations, it is impossible to give you guidance as to the likely number of words required for each section. However, as Chapter Ten on assessment makes clear, there are particular areas that are regarded as of paramount importance and are therefore likely to require a greater number of words. These are likely to be the Results and Analysis section(s), the Literature and the Methodology. We stress that *all* sections are important, but for candidates who come into the 'borderline' category, these sections especially should not be skimped and those seeking a Grade A will seek to ensure these are of the highest quality. We mention the length of sections for guidance only; it is of little use writing an Introduction section of, say, 5,000 words, and giving your Analysis section fewer than that when it is obvious at this level that the latter is far more important.

Submitting your proposal for approval

At some point, you will be required to submit an actual proposal for your project or dissertation. This will need to be approved by your supervisor or, occasionally, by a group or committee. Although details may change during the course of your research, the proposal needs to be clear and should cover the following:

- A provisional title – usually known as a 'working title'
- A statement about the purpose and aims of the project
- A statement indicating what you see as the value of your research, especially in terms of the institution(s) it affects
- An overview of the methodologies proposed
- An indication of some key reading i.e. main literature texts likely to be used
- A statement about how you will ensure confidentiality of participants (Note: sometimes, a separate statement is required covering the ethical procedures involved, which has to be approved; see Chapter Five for a detailed discussion of ethical procedures)
- An outline work schedule for yourself leading to the proposed completion date.

Sometimes, a proposal pro forma is required to be completed (see Chapter Ten for an example); alternatively you may be asked for a proposal statement of a specified number of words. The format above will cover the normal requirements.

Understanding the main research approaches and designing your research

Let us start by reflecting on what we actually mean by research. Bassey (1999: 38) defines it as being a 'systematic, critical and self-critical inquiry which aims to contribute to the advancement of knowledge and wisdom'. Johnson (1994: 3) calls it a 'focused and systematic enquiry that goes beyond generally available knowledge to acquire specialised and detailed information, providing a basis for analysis and elucidatory comment on the topic of enquiry'.

These two definitions give a common-sense perspective of what you are trying to achieve. You are attempting to enquire in a systematic way into a particular topic; this will give you data which, when analysed, will provide new information about the topic chosen. You may care to use these as a checklist of criteria whilst carrying out your project. Especially during periods perhaps when you feel little progress is being made or the project is going 'off track', ask yourself whether it is systematic, whether you are being self-critical and whether the data you are collecting will be a good basis for analysis.

There are a number of different traditions in approaches to research and it is easy to feel overwhelmed by the vocabulary used in some texts in describing these (words such as 'ontological' 'epistemological' and 'axiological' can be intimidating!). At Masters Level, you need to remember that you are not a career professional researcher, but you do need a clear understanding of the main paradigms. We consider these now, relatively briefly, and then ask you to reflect on whether you are primarily suited to a particular one.

Originally, the 'scientific' method favoured by the natural sciences was seen as the superior form of research; gradually the developments in social sciences meant that contrasting forms of research were seen as the most valid in particular fields. We shall try to summarise these two main paradigms although they overlap, as you will see, with others.

- *Positivism*: This is often known as the quantitative paradigm and basically tries to adopt the 'scientific' approach. This means there is an insistence on objectivity, the collection of facts and the acceptance that only these provide 'real' knowledge. People's feelings therefore cannot be accepted as evidence. Critics such as Popper (1968) and Crotty (1998) have argued that positivism should not be seen as simplistically as this, because science itself is increasingly less certain, but it is clear that some of its approaches, especially its insistence on empirical investigation, have been of enduring value.
- *Interpretivism*: This is known as the qualitative paradigm and sometimes you will find the term 'relativism' used. As its name suggests, this paradigm is about how people interpret or have interpreted the world around them. The focus therefore is on the individual and his/her view of the social situation(s), including relationships.

In discussing these two paradigms, it is easy to become drawn into discussions about what is 'truth' and what is 'reality'. However, unless you are studying philosophy, such debates can be distracting from your actual research purpose. Perhaps we can best illustrate the contrasting approaches through actual examples from Masters students' work.

Case example 2.1

Daisy, who worked in tourism and was taking a Masters in Business Studies, and Oliver, a secondary school teacher studying for a Masters in Educational Leadership were both interested in the same broad topic. This was to investigate whether perceptions of praise given for performance by 'managers' to 'workers' were different according to the givers and recipients of the praise. In Oliver's case, he wondered why teachers appeared to be clear that they had been giving praise to pupils in class, whilst many pupils felt they were *not* praised for their work. Similarly, Daisy had noticed that workers in the offices said that managers hardly ever praised them for their work but were quick to criticise.

Oliver wanted to explore this issue in the context of pupil motivation, so his topic was 'To what extent can pupil motivation be improved by the effective use of leaders' praise and rewards?' whilst Daisy set her interest in the context of work morale and asked 'To what extent is staff morale affected by the effective use of praise by management?'

The quantitative approach to these situations is that the reality is that either praise is given or it is not. By establishing how many times praise is given, the situation becomes clear. Through observation or some enumerating strategy, for example counting the number of written commendations or memoranda, the 'truth' can be arrived at.

The qualitative approach is that people's perceptions of the praise they receive is what is important. For example, a recipient might regard a piece of praise as tokenistic or insincere and therefore reject it as not being 'true' praise.

Both Daisy and Oliver, in their different contexts, actually carried out a mixture of quantitative and qualitative methods in their research (these are dealt with fully in Chapter Four). Each discovered that the 'truth' lay in both areas! Managers and leaders *had* given praise, but the recipients, even when faced with the data about the number of times they had been praised, did not always acknowledge that their praise was 'true' or helpful!

This combining of the two approaches is widely used, as we shall see.

Positivist Paradigm	Interpretivist Paradigm
• Value free	• Human interests and interpretations
• Observer is independent	• Observer is 'a party' to the action
• Focused on facts	• Focused on interpretations
• Quantitative methods	• Qualitative methods
• Precise measurement	• Different perceptions gained

Figure 2.2 Contrasting positivist and interpretivist paradigms (based on Easterby-Smith et al., 2002)

Whichever approach is used, certain features of the 'scientific' approach remain essential to good research. As well as the emphasis on empirical work, mentioned above, notions of being precise in measuring something for evaluation and keeping meticulously accurate records are essential for all research.

Figure 2.2 summarises the essential differences between the two main paradigms we have considered, so that you can then reflect on which one is more suitable for you personally and for your research in your chosen topic.

Some of the issues arising from this enable us to note that there are different implications for the way you carry out your research in each approach. An essentially quantitative approach will:

- Provide data about a larger population
- Be quicker to administer once the instruments are prepared carefully
- Provide data which is relatively straightforward to analyse (software may be needed for large-scale population data).

An essentially qualitative approach will:

- Provide rich or 'thick' evidence or descriptions of the feelings and perceptions of a relatively small number of people
- Take longer to administer as each person or group needs an equal focus of attention
- Ensure that basic resources are all that are necessary for a relatively small population
- Enable instruments to be refined and adjusted should circumstances require it.

In addition, James et al. (2008: 60) state that with a qualitative approach, 'Should the first analysis not work out, data can be re-examined to draw out a more convincing argument; the data either present a convincing story or they do not'.

We suggest that, with your knowledge of the main research paradigms and your experience from your previous assignments during your Masters programme, you should be in a position to consider your own abilities and preferences in helping to decide upon the approach which is most suitable for you and for your chosen topic.

The following questions can be asked of yourself:

- Which of the two sets of assumptions behind the main paradigms am I more comfortable with?
- Are my writing skills primarily of the technical kind or more 'literary'?
- Have I shown and enjoyed computer statistical skills or text analysis skills?
- Do I prefer fairly rigid rules in constructing research or do I prefer looser guidelines?
- Do I have a low tolerance, even dislike, of ambiguity or do I have a high tolerance for ambiguity, accepting a less than clear outcome?
- Do I prefer working on a 'constant' regardless of context or do I enjoy understanding and building up a picture of the context within which people operate?

The first alternatives in all the above tend toward the quantitative paradigm and the second towards the qualitative. We might add one further consideration and that is the audience for whom you are carrying out this research and to whom you will be presenting your final report. Of course, you have to satisfy your HE institution assessors first of all, but many of you will be supported or sponsored by an employer. These employers are supportive of your studies; are they in any way more likely to be persuaded of the worth and relevance of your work-based project if it is more quantitatively or qualitatively focused? It is worth reflecting for a while at least, perhaps even sharing these with work colleagues.

At the beginning of this chapter, we stated clearly how important it is to choose a topic that interests you. We would now add a further 'golden rule':

Choose a topic and an approach where you can most effectively use the skills which you have.

Finally, in this section, we have tried to describe research approaches in a non-technical way, but here are a few words which you may encounter.

Axiology – this means the study of values

Epistemology – this is concerned with the nature of knowledge and how knowledge is acquired and validated

Grounded theory – this involves deriving theories and models from the data as they are acquired, rather than drawing on existing theories
Ontology – concerns the nature of existence, the world, reality.

Case study research

You will have already encountered case study research during your Masters programme and may well have developed a case study for an assignment. Almost certainly, you will have read various case studies. However, it is worth examining in detail the possibilities of case study research for your final project and being aware of the advantages and disadvantages of adopting this particular approach. Please note that throughout this book, we use Case *Examples* to illustrate a point, not case studies which we now discuss.

Case studies are a valuable way of carrying out research for part-time students at Masters Level, who are also employees in other roles and have limited opportunities in terms of time and resources. A case study is an enquiry which focuses on a specific situation, unit, or group (or even an individual person). This unit may be an institution such as a company or a school, or a sub-unit, such as a local branch of business or a department in a college, for example. Various definitions of case study include:

> ...an enquiry which uses multiple sources of evidence. It investigates a contemporary phenomenon within its real-life context... (Johnson, 1994: 20)

> The purpose [of case study] is to probe deeply and to analyse intensively the multifarious phenomena that constitute the life cycle of the unit... (Cohen and Manion, 2000: 106)

> an umbrella term for a family of research methods having in common the decision to focus an enquiry around an instance. (Adelman et al., 1984: 94)

> an empirical enquiry that investigates a contemporary phenomenon. (Yin, 2003: 13)

Key words from these definitions tell you that a case study:

- Is current
- Is specific
- Is focused
- Is detailed
- Uses a variety of research methods.

While each case study is specific, research often uses what is known as 'multiple case studies'. In the reality of Masters Level research work, 'multiple' is likely to mean in practical terms three or four at the most. In other words, let us say three units may be studied in depth. Each has something in common, such as being a school or a department or a business office. Comparisons and contrasts are then able to be made across the data from all three case studies enabling conclusions to be drawn, which *may* offer possible generalisations for that type of unit. We say 'may' because the issue of generalisation is one of the criticisms levelled at case study research.

Possible problems in case study research include:

- The uniqueness of the study means that it can be difficult to generalise the findings to wider applications. It can be argued that using multiple case studies reduces this risk to some extent.
- A very large amount of data such as documentation can be generated.
- Some critics believe it lacks rigour because there are no set rules as each case is specific.
- Researchers sometimes find they are given different access by different people to particular sources of data, both within one unit and sometimes between different units. One student, studying development planning in primary schools in a small island state, found that in one of his three case study schools, the key document had been mislaid. He was never able to access it.

However, there are considerable strengths in case study research:

- It is very relevant to Masters Level students, and, as Nisbett and Watt (1984: 76) suggest 'particularly suited to the individual researcher'.
- Case studies provide very 'rich' descriptions of events or situations.
- Case studies are very understandable to the readers of reports because people can relate to them.
- Case studies show that 'truth' or 'reality' are indeed complex, as they often provide alternative interpretations.
- Above all, they are essentially 'real' because they deal with actual situations or institutional contexts.

Types of case study

Bassey (2002: 111–14) suggests that case studies can:

- Draw a picture' of the unit concerned, through rich description
- Be evaluative
- Test out a theory or seek to develop a theory.

The latter of these two may be more likely when multiple case studies have been researched.

How do we select a case study?

If you have decided on a case study approach to researching the chosen topic, you may consider one of these types of unit group institution or situation for a case study, as Lichtman (2009) suggests.

(a) You may choose a *typical* case. If, for example, you decide to research the impact of leaders' mentoring on primary teachers' class performance, you will select a teacher and class which you see as typical. You will need to set criteria, such as a class which has attainment similar to that of the school as a whole. If multiple case studies are used, all such classes would need to be typical.

(b) You may choose an *exemplary* model. Here you select a unit which is seen as offering best practice in its field. For example, you might select the local branch of a national tourism business which has won the most awards for its service and investigate the factors which appear to have contributed to its success.

(c) A third option is to select an *unusual* or *special* case. Here, for example, you may be interested, in a unit where the vast majority of the employees are female in a business or company which is male-dominated – or vice versa. This special case *may* indicate some of the ways in which this has occurred and what impact, if any, it has had on performance.

Carrying out case study research

Details of actual research methods and their application are fully dealt with in Chapters Four and Five, but the actual stages of conducting the case study research are suggested by Bassey (2002: 115) as:

1. Identify the purpose
2. Ask research questions
3. Establish ethical guidelines
4. Collect and store data
5. Generate and test analytical statements
6. Interpret these statements
7. Decide conclusions, write report, disseminate.

With case studies, because they are so individual and personal, it is well worth asking someone objective, a critical friend, to examine your report and conclusions. It is very easy to get drawn unwillingly into what we call over-familiarity with the situation which is being researched. You are likely to make several visits to the institution, and become known and get to know the people there. An external perspective can therefore be invaluable in seeing if you have become 'too close'.

Overall, case study research, despite some of its limitations, is a very popular and credible approach for many students in leadership and management because of the inherent value and accessibility which it usually offers.

Comparative research and the importance of culture and context

All research takes place in specific contexts, normally within a single country or region. However, we need to consider what is involved in research for those students who wish to use their experience and understanding of more than one country as the basis for some kind of comparative research. For example, you may be a student who is studying in one country for your Masters Degree but grew up and was educated in another. You may be or have been involved in a secondment or cultural exchange between two countries, or perhaps have merely visited another country on a professional basis and have contacts you feel you can use. Since the 1980s there has developed a much greater awareness of and sensitivity towards different cultures, and therefore the scope for such comparative research is now considerable. That awareness and sensitivity needs to be displayed by any student in carrying out such research.

There are several sound reasons for carrying out this type of comparative research:

- Comparison is an essential part of all research anyway. 'Comparison can help us to understand, to extend our insights and to sharpen our perspectives. If we wish to know something well ... comparison is integral to the process of cognition and perhaps all human thought. ... Thinking without comparison is unthinkable'. (Theisen and Adams, 1990: 277)
- We live now in a global society and there is huge and essential reciprocal interest between, for example, East and West in the fields of finance, business, education and public services.
- The more we know about our own and other societies, the more we learn about ourselves and our own society, so research here can contribute much on both a personal and institutional scale.

Understanding different cultures and contexts: issues to consider

We are all conditioned by our own culture and something for the researcher to avoid is to find oneself transposing one's own values and viewpoints onto a different culture or context. Bush and Middlewood (2005) explore several examples in terms of people management of how practices differ widely in different cultures. For example, they point out that 'whilst gender, for example, may be treated as an equal opportunities issue in Western societies, it is a more complex phenomenon in segregated societies and in patriarchal and collective societies where motherhood and age are equated with status and authority' (2005: 98). They also point to different approaches to work, mentioning:

- Japanese group ethic
- Chinese work ethic
- African collaborative approaches
- Western problem-solving abilities.

As writers such as Dimmock (2002) have pointed out, Western research literature in leadership and management for a long time tended to transpose Western values onto Eastern or African contexts in analysis without taking account of the inherent differences between them, each culture having its own intrinsic approach and traditions.

Attitudes to researchers

Some cultures are far more deferential or assertive than others and this can have an impact on how research methods are received. For example, questions which challenge the superiority of someone with managerial status can be viewed as ill-mannered in some societies, and the status of a teacher in some faith-based cultures has to remain beyond question.

In some cultures, it is considered impolite to refuse or simply say 'no' so that closed questions can lead to various complications!

Language issues

This of course can be a matter of translation or mistranslation, with all its potential for misinterpretation. Should you operate in a research context where at any point an interpreter is needed, you need to note in your report that this was the case and therefore you cannot vouch for the interpretation being a 100% accurate. Thus, Bush, Qiang and Fang (1998: 135–6) note in their report on management research in China:

> The language difficulty meant that the Chinese partner acted as interpreter in order to convey questions to interviewees and responses to the English researcher. The authors [of the report] acknowledge the potential for misunderstanding and possible inaccuracy in interpreting and recording the comments of participants.

Clearly, dialect differences within countries can also make for some potential misunderstandings. One of the authors of this book found that one or two key words related to 'performance' were interpreted differently between the

Greek mainland and the Greek islands, which caused initial misinterpretation in recording the views of participants.

Differences within countries

As with dialect, differences between different regions of the same country are often quite marked, so it is unrealistic, especially in larger countries, to talk of a single culture. By 'larger' here, we tend to mean in geographical terms, rather than by population. Even in a highly centralised system, where the country is large, the attitude in rural areas very distant from the urban 'headquarters' may be quite distinct. Again, in a part of one of the Greek islands, one researcher found that the attitude to the national system of appraisal was based on the firm belief that 'we don't take much notice of what happens in the capital; nobody ever comes here to check!' (Middlewood, 2001: 184).

Similarly, Bush, Qiang and Fang (1998: 137) said that, although they researched in a range of schools, the 'county is too large and diverse for the authors (of the report) to be confident that the findings can be generalised to other parts of the country'.

Which approach to use in other countries?

It is likely that, given limited time in a different country, the researcher may find the use of individual case studies to be valuable. Large-scale surveys are more likely to be deficient in detail, unless the context is known extremely well. Therefore, qualitative research, according to writers such as Theisen and Adams (1990), is likely to be most effective in carrying out comparative research, especially perhaps in developing countries.

Drawing out conclusions from comparative research

Having noted the need for awareness of and sensitivity towards the inherent nature of each specific culture and even the differences within countries, the researcher needs to ensure the actual purpose of the research is crystal clear. It clearly will not be to emphasise the superiority of one system to another, as, if it is an evaluative study, it may only assess effectiveness in each specific context. It may, however, attempt to discover the elements within each system that are common and try to pose questions as to how they work well or not – and why – in each context. Although the conclusions may be cautious, there is a great deal to be gained from research in contrasting cultures. Such research should be of interest to both cultures and, possibly, especially in business, increase the opportunities for enhancing links with different countries, based on the understanding that the research has demonstrated.

Summary of Chapter Two

This chapter has:

- Described and discussed the factors that you need to consider in deciding upon the topic for your final project
- Described the structure that is likely to be needed for your final report
- Described and discussed the main research approaches which you should consider in designing your research
- Described the use of case studies, looked at the different kinds, and considered their applicability and suitability
- Given advice about what needs to be taken into account when considering comparative international research.

Further reading

Gray, D. (2009) *Doing Research in the Real World*, 2nd edn. London: Sage.

Yin, R. (2003) *Case Study Research: Design and Methods*, 3rd edn. Thousands Oaks, CA: Sage.

3

The Literature Review

Introduction

In the previous chapter we looked at the issues surrounding your choice of research topic. One of the key factors to consider in your choice of topic will have been the availability of relevant literature and access to research sources. A wide range of literature will provide you with a good foundation to build on as you progress through your chosen project area. An appropriate amount and range of literature will enable you to develop a coherent argument and to compare the findings from your research project with those of other researchers and official publications. Ensuring access to literature is a key issue and you will need to decide what constitutes relevant literature for your particular project. Given the information explosion we have experienced in recent years, some of your time will be spent on deciding what is appropriate literature. The internet is a valuable and useful resource in accessing literature. However, given the scope of your project, you have to be realistic about the amount of literature you can use. In most cases an excess rather than a shortage of literature is likely to be the problem, and you will need to develop the ability to be selective about the literature you use. You will need to develop skills which will enable you to make the most of the available literature in your chosen area. This chapter will consider the scope and role of the literature review in your project and the following topics are addressed:

- The purpose of your literature review
- The overall structure of the review
- Different types of literature
- Using online materials

- Making use of official publications
- Using literature from within your organisation
- Developing critical analysis.

Purpose of the literature review

Whatever the extent of the literature, which at times might appear daunting, hopefully you will have chosen a topic for your project that you have a genuine interest in and commitment to. Your choice of topic should also have a positive impact on your professional practice. The reading that you have to undertake should therefore be beneficial for your career, enjoyable and not be seen as a chore. At times you might find yourself thinking 'Not another research report to read!', but, as we have written in earlier chapters, the project gives you the opportunity to develop a deep understanding of a topic. By the time you come to submit your project you should be an expert in your chosen field. Hopefully by the end of the process you will also still have retained your initial enthusiasm for the topic you have chosen to investigate.

Your project literature review plays a significant part in demonstrating your knowledge of the subject area and provides you with an opportunity to display your skills of analysis and reflection. Missing a significant publication or failing to properly interrogate the literature will lead to serious problems later and create a number of questions about your overall approach during the assessment of your project. You have to use a wide range of relevant sources, show that you understand them, interrogate them critically and employ them to support the arguments you are making. However, it is important that you make the most of the available literature and you may use one key source in a number of different parts of your project. Do not rely on one text, but there might be a seminal work that you have to refer to a number of times. You also have to ensure that the literature you use is relevant and up to date and you need to ensure that your literature is sufficiently detailed to cover the various aspects of your project.

At Masters Level you must adopt a critical approach and merely describing the literature is not sufficient. Analysis is at the heart of what you are doing and you have to set the literature in the broader context and draw on a wide range of viewpoints and perspectives. So, getting this part of your project right from the outset is important and will set the tone for the project as a whole.

The literature review is a major part of your final submission and is designed to fulfil a number of purposes:

- To provide a background context for your project and area of investigation
- To broaden your knowledge and understanding of the subject area

- To provide a rationale for your project
- To enable you to display a thorough understanding of the subject area through utilising a range of relevant sources
- To display your knowledge and understanding of the subject area
- To give you the opportunity to analyse and critique a range of literature relevant to your study
- To compare different theoretical approaches
- To develop ideas and approaches that will be useful in carrying out your project.

The literature review will provide you with a range of material to enable you to begin your project. You will start to collect references and quotes and these can be used to develop your own ideas and questions. Your initial reading of the literature has to be focused and purposeful and you will need to extract information and material that might be useful from the various sources you access. These may include:

- Factual information
- Definitions of key terms
- Theories
- Concepts
- Research findings
- Relevant quotations.

The 'golden rule' here is:

> Your literature review has to be focused, purposeful and offer a critique.

The structure of the review

In your earlier assignments you will have carried out a limited literature review, often to set the context and to display key ideas. The general approach you were recommended to follow remains the same in your project, but this literature review has to be on a larger scale and contain greater analysis. The importance of consulting a wide range of source material is extremely important and it gives you the opportunity to display your knowledge and understanding of the subject matter. However, merely creating a long list of sources and describing them is not enough at Masters Level. Do not make the mistake of thinking you have to include everything that has ever been written on your topic. You have to make sure that the majority of your project does not turn into a review of the literature. You have to manage the process properly and adopt a questioning approach in order to offer a critique of the relevant material. In the past you may have had feedback from your tutor on previous written work that 'it was too descriptive' or 'lacking in critical analysis'. So, what does this mean in practice?

Developing a critical approach requires you to start by reading a wide range of material critically. In particular, you have to adopt a critical approach by questioning the material, for example by comparing it to other material you have read.

- Does it support or differ from the other material you have consulted?
- Are there recurring themes and findings, and are there any connections to other work?
- You will need to provide evidence that can be utilised to support or rebut assertions and identify contradictions and conflict. You will also have to consider the methods used by the authors:

  o What are the strengths and weaknesses of the approach they have identified?
  o How have the authors arrived at their findings?
  o In particular what assumptions have they made to reach their conclusions?

- Issues such as sample size and the basis of their evidence are all issues you need to consider in a critical manner. You cannot accept material at face value and you must question what has been written even if the author is a leading expert in the field or it is an official publication! Developing a critical approach to your reading will enable you to start out on the literature review in the right way.

We have already pointed out that you need to make sure you have consulted a sufficient number of relevant sources that provide a good coverage of your chosen topic area. Later in the chapter we will discuss in detail the various types of material you can drawn on, but you will need to use:

- Books
- Book chapters
- Journal articles
- Government publications
- Reports
- Professional publications
- Web-based resources
- Documents from your own organisation.

Identifying the range of material will be dependent on your own particular topic area, and the focus of your project. Your tutor will be able to provide guidance and support on your initial reading. Once you have started on this process you will find that you will discover other material that will take you in different directions, but always remember the 'golden rule' (above).

One good way of starting the literature review is to consider materials in chronological order. This will enable you to see how ideas have developed over time and to compare different materials. However, you have to be realistic about how far in time you can go back. You also have to remember that you are likely to be investigating an area that is experiencing rapid change, so be careful not to spend too much time on the historical context. Whilst it is important to display your knowledge of the subject area, ensure that your choice of literature is relevant to your particular project. Too often students want to include everything, but you have to be selective and critical.

Another way of starting the process is to identify a seminal publication that is considered to be the basis for the area you are investigating. This might be an official or government publication that establishes the framework for work in the area you are investigating. This will provide a springboard into the rest of the literature and for your project as a whole. Alternatively you might decide to begin with a definition of your chosen topic area, break it down into a number of areas and relate the literature to each of the areas you have identified.

We can illustrate different approaches to the literature review by considering some examples from actual student projects:

Case example 3.1

Olga, a manager in an HE institution in Kazakhstan, decided to investigate the impact on managers of the introduction of a credit system into an HE institution in Kazakhstan. Her literature review was structured on a chronological basis:

- HE policies during the Soviet period of government
- Independence and the modern era in Kazakhstan
- General economic and educational reform post-1991
- Specific HE development and reform in Kazakhstan post-1991
- Development of leadership and management in HE in Kazakhstan post-1991.

Underlying principles and policies:

- Reforms in HE: development and implementation of the credit system
- Training and development for leaders and managers responsible for putting the credit system into practice.

Case example 3.2

Manjit, a deputy headteacher in a secondary school in the UK, had chosen to research 'Leading and managing effective staff recruitment and selection'. His literature review was structured around definitions of key terms:

A. *What is recruitment and selection?*

- Part of the process of staff management
- The difference between recruitment and selection
- Criteria for effectiveness.

B. *What is involved in recruitment?*

- Contexts and considerations
- Potential problems.

C. *What is involved in selection?*

- Contexts and consideration
- Potential problems.

D. *Who should be involved?*

- Role of school leaders
- Role of governors and other stakeholders
- Issues of training and development.

E. *Assessing the effectiveness of the process*

- Reviewing the appointee's performance
- Reviewing the actual processes.

Different types of literature

You may also need to look at a variety of types of literature and you might decide to structure your literature review on this basis. In particular you will look at a range of sources and these will include:

- *Policy based literature* is directed at a particular initiative that the government or official organisation is implementing. You will need to draw on this to show that you have a grasp of current developments in your field. However, you have to bear in mind that policy based literature is not neutral and will reflect the ideology of the government or official organisation responsible for the development of the policy. By definition, this type of literature will tend to be partisan and present a particular perspective. Although this type of literature comes with official approval you should make sure you question it in the normal way. You may not be able to change the policy, it might impact on you directly and you might disagree with the impact of the implementation, but you have to interrogate it fully.

- *Research based literature* provides a written account of a particular research project. Normally it will have been carried out by an established academic team who have been commissioned by a funding body to conduct the research. It can take the form of a research report which will then provide the basis for the majority of academic papers. Peer reviewed literature has the highest academic authority, but that does not mean that you should be afraid to question this type of literature. You need to consider the methodology that the researchers have employed to accumulate the data and to look at who has funded the research. Remember that there is good and bad research and part of your task in your Masters Level project is to show an awareness of the range and quality of research in your field.

- *Theory based literature* will be part of any research based literature you look at. The way theory based literature is incorporated in research based literature will provide a guide to how you might use it in your project. You can use this type of literature to support your own arguments, but you cannot just reproduce the theory. As with all literature you have to adopt a critical approach and interrogate it fully. If you are investigating a particular policy development this is likely to have been based on a particular theory. The theoretical literature will provide you with a useful starting point as you go on to look at the implications of the particular policy you are investigating.

- *Review based literature* will adopt a critical perspective and put forward different points of view. A significant amount of literature will be based on a review of the existing literature or is a review of relevant research. In a sense, this is what you are attempting to do in the literature review in your project. Review based research will give you access to a wide range of sources and authors who have written on your topic. You will need to take this type of literature as a starting point and it will provide a number of potential avenues for you to explore as you develop your own literature review.

- *Practice based literature* is increasing in popularity because it is based on actual practice in your own area of work. We will return to this as a specific research method in Chapter Six when we look at practitioner research. This type of literature is growing in popularity because it is directly linked to what people do in their workplace and is based on real-life experience. There is a strong desire for research to be perceived as useful and related to the real world. This type of literature is primarily concerned with improving practice and success is dependent on effective reflection by the practitioner. The literature may be based around what appears to be mundane and common practice in the workplace, but the key feature is critical reflection and how the author uses this to improve practice.

- *Normative literature.* This type of literature is very tempting but should be treated with caution. A great number of books can be found which are not based on any research or real evidence at all but are merely the writers' views, drawing usually on their own experience. For example, in Case Example 3.2, Manjit was able to find many books which tell you how to find the best people to employ, written by successful and often well-known leaders and managers in business or politics. They have formed their opinions and believe that THIS (i.e. their) way is the best way to proceed. Their experience may be valuable and can sometimes provide a useful quotation, as long as you recognise their limitations in that the statements and assertions lack research and real evidence.

- *Methodology based literature* will be used to justify your choice of research methods. You will use the literature to interrogate the research methods you have chosen to use to gather your data. You will need to discuss the positive and negative aspects of your data collection and show that you are aware of any issues raised by your choice of research methodology.

A great deal of the literature you use during your project will contain elements of all of the variety of literature we have just described. For example, research based literature will have elements of theory based literature and might be based on a research project based on practice in the workplace.

Using the literature

You are likely to use a range of literature from different sources as you construct your literature review. As part of the assessment of your project you will need to show that you have used a range of source material. At the outset it is worth developing good habits to save time later on. You need to establish procedures to maintain a record of what you are reading. There is nothing more frustrating than having to search for missing page numbers or titles when you are trying to finish off the project. Make sure you have a system in place that enables you to record this information and allows you to cite references properly by following the accepted guidelines. If you fail to do this, you may be accused of plagiarism. So, keep precise details of any direct quotations you might use. Adopt a system for you that works and you feel comfortable with. Some of you will use IT to do this while others will rely on the old fashioned pen and paper approach. Whatever method you decide to utilise remember to get into the habit of being consistent and maintaining up-to-date details of material you have used.

In addition to direct quotations you will also paraphrase literature you have read and you must also record this information. Let us take an example to illustrate how you might paraphrase a particular piece of material. In this example, the original quotation is:

National governments, and politicians generally, continue to clamour for improved educational performance as a key to improving economic prosperity in their countries. Regularly published educational tables of comparative attainments, usually test results at certain ages, indicate clearly this emphasis – and thereby the pressure – placed on the educational institutions and their leaders to regularly raise the standards, that is, measurable attainment of pupils and students. Schools are often the institutions most stressed in these comparisons because, although in developed countries post-statutory education, including at university level, is also subject to comparison, there is no doubt that governments place most emphasis on performance during statutory school age because of the huge investments in this area. Public scrutiny is therefore greatest in this field. (Middlewood, 2010: 132)

You could paraphrase this example by writing:

Middlewood (2010) claims that schools face the brunt of government policies designed to raise educational standards, in an attempt to improve economic performance, and are likely to be the subject of a complex range of techniques to measure student achievement.

Which types of publication will you use?

The type of literature you use will to some extent depend on your choice of topic, but it has to have sufficient breadth and, of course, be relevant. You are likely to use: books, chapters, journal articles, official reports from government or professional associations, legislation including White Papers and Acts of Parliament, internal documents from organisations, and magazines and newspapers. Some of these materials will be in traditional printed format, but increasingly many will be web-based. As you are involved in writing an academic piece of work the emphasis is likely to be on academic literature. However, your project may be more professionally based and you will need to include literature from this aspect too.

Literature written for different audiences and purposes will vary in quality and have different academic validity. You will not be able to base your literature review solely on newspaper and magazine articles, but they can be useful to indicate, for example, the strength of feeling about a particular topic or to provide quotes from prominent individuals. In education and business, for example, you will find that a huge amount is written in the quality press about recent policy developments. You have to be selective and to accept that even if you find a large amount of material on your topic in newspapers and magazines you can only use a small amount from this source in your project.

At Masters Level, academic articles from peer reviewed journals, closely followed by books and chapters, have the highest degree of acceptance, and you will need to show that you are able to use these to develop your project. Even if your project is more professionally based you will still need to draw on academic sources as well as the professional and organisation based literature that you might use. If your project is related to a major piece of legislation you will need to draw on this, and to show that you understand the official literature. Hopefully the legislation has been developed on the basis of some academic underpinning and you will need to explore this as well for the particular policy you are interested in.

The temptation for many students when they are doing their literature review is to quote extensively, partly because it is a good way of quickly working away at the word total. However, this is not the best approach and you have to use quotations sparingly and as a means to illuminate your arguments. You have to show that you are using quotations as a means of developing a well-focused relevant argument as part of your project, rather than a form of 'padding' to reach the word total. Always remember to adopt a critical, questioning approach to any form of literature and to use direct quotations sparingly to illustrate the point you are making.

Using online materials

In recent years the biggest development relating to the literature review has been the amount of material available on the internet. If you carry out a search for your chosen topic you will probably get a huge number of responses. Given the scope of your Masters Level project it would be impossible to include everything, and, as we have already pointed out, that is not the purpose of the literature review. Given the limitations of your project, what online materials should you use?

Many of the traditional sources we have already mentioned will be available on the internet, but these are not specifically online materials. However, there will be particular websites that you might decide to access where information is only available online. To be acceptable for a Masters Level project these have to be official or reputable academic websites. For example, if your project is based on aspects of leadership in health and safety in business you might need to look at the website of the Department for Business, Innovation and Skills (BIS). After looking at that website you may go to the website for the Health and Safety Executive, and so on. If you are looking at aspects of leadership in education a starting point might be the website of the Department for Education (DfE) and from there your search might lead to the National College for Leadership of Schools and Children's Services (NCSL). Your choice of topic will lead the way in determining the websites you use, but in the limited examples we have given all the examples are official websites and are considered to be acceptable sources in a Masters Level project.

There will also be academic resources that are only available online and these will vary from subject to subject. Many journals and even books are moving to online publishing. Your library and project tutor will be able to provide specific details of these for your subject area, but there are certain basic questions to ask when you are consulting academic resources online:

- Is the material based on research findings?
- Does the material have any official credibility? For example, is it research commissioned for government or an official body?
- Has the material been externally (peer) reviewed by members of the academic community?
- What is the status of the website on which the material is available?

You will have to evaluate what is acceptable because the quality of online materials does vary. Even long established sources such as Wikipedia are not accepted as an academic source, although it might provide you with a useful pointer to other more acceptable sources. Your choice of online materials has to stand up to the normal tests for any literature you decide to include in your project, but unlike the traditional printed format, online materials can change over time as websites do disappear and are updated. You should make sure you print a copy of the material and keep the web page electronically in case it is deleted or changed. Finally keep a record of the URL (web address) and the date when you looked at the material.

Making use of official publications

You will almost certainly need to make some use of official publications as part of your Masters Level project. Official publications will provide a context and detailed information about the particular area you are investigating. In many cases official publications will provide the starting point for your investigation. This is true in both the public and private sectors. The topic you are investigating may have been introduced as a piece of legislation by national or local government. Once the enabling legislation has been put in place official bodies may also produce guidance material that sets out how the policy will work in practice. If, for example, your topic was based around leadership issues in relation to employment rights in your organisation, then a good starting point in the UK would be to look at the publications of the Department for Business, Innovation and Skills. A publication such as: 'Want to Know More about your Rights at Work? You Have a Powerful Friend', would provide you with a good outline of the area and the legislation relating to this area (BIS, 2010).

Using this type of publication only gives you factual information that you can use as a starting point. You will need to search further to see if there have been reports on the impact of the various policies and how they have been implemented. You also have to take into account the perspective of the organisation providing this information. For example, a government department will want to present the best possible picture of any of their policies. This does not invalidate the data, but you have to fully interrogate the data and not accept it at face value, even if carries official approval.

Even when seemingly independent organisations produce official publications you have to retain the same degree of scepticism. For example, in education, the Office for Standards in Education (Ofsted) produce a huge number of reports and documents about the standard of education provision in England. Ofsted claims to be an independent organisation and places great emphasis on its impartiality (Ofsted, 2009). However, their findings are not always universally accepted, are subject to scrutiny and there are often questions raised about their choice of methodology. When you access official publications you have to ask:

- What perspective is it written from?
- Who has gathered the data?
- Who has written the material?
- Who is the potential audience?
- Why has it been written?
- What status does it have?
- What methodology was used?
- Are there alternative viewpoints from other individuals/organisations?

Using literature from within your own organisation

If you are a part-time student or have been seconded to study for your Masters Level qualification you might decide to base your project on your own organisation. If your project is based on an issue in your own organisation or a case study you will need to draw on internal literature. This type of material is clearly not produced for an academic or external audience, but it can still be used in your project, especially as part of your background work and to illustrate key concepts. However, it should not constitute the bulk of your literature review and wherever possible should be used alongside more traditional academic sources. If you do decide to use material from within your own organisation there are a number of issues you need to consider:

- *Access*: You are an employee of the organisation so you might assume access to internal literature is not an issue. However, your managers may not want to give you access to all the relevant documentation you might need. Make sure you have clearance from senior managers about access and how you can use any material when you are writing up your project.
- *Confidentiality*: Internal literature is written for use within the organisation and it might contain information that should not be seen externally. There could be a number of reasons for this including restricting information that would be beneficial to competitors or details about particular individuals. Make sure you establish clear protocols about the type of internal material you can use in your project and be sensitive to the needs of the organisation.
- *Purpose*: Remember that literature from your own organisation was written with a particular purpose in mind and for a specific audience. The literature might contain language that has a specific meaning in the organisation or might be directed at particular categories of staff. Given your internal knowledge you will be clear about what has been written, but outsiders will not have the same level of insight. If this is the case, you will need to explain this in your literature review otherwise this could create the potential for misunderstanding when the project is read and assessed.
- *Context*: You are familiar with the context of your organisation, but others will not have the benefit of your experience and insight. Remember to explain the broader context and background of the organisation and the particular context of any internal literature you decide to use.
- *Anonymity*: This might be a condition of access to internal literature, but it is normally good practice to change the names of any organisation or individuals you include in your project. This can become more difficult when you are referring to internal documents, so make sure you adopt a consistent and rigorous approach.
- *Conflict of interest*: You must explain if you have had any role in developing and writing the internal literature you are using. You must also outline how the particular literature has impacted on you or your practice and justify your interpretation.

Developing critical analysis

By far the most important aspect of your Masters Level project is your capacity to develop critical analysis. We have already briefly considered this earlier in the chapter and it is a theme we will return to at a number of points in future chapters. However, we will now identify the key components of effective critical analysis when you are carrying out your literature review.

As a starting point you have to develop the capacity to read critically. This appears to be an obvious statement, but given the amount of literature available there is a temptation to fall into the trap of reading and accepting information at face value. Many students think there is an acceptable number of references that tutors are looking for, and once they have reached that number then everything is fine. You have to include the key texts, but it is not a numbers game and you need to be selective about what to include in your project.

At Masters Level you cannot read material in a passive manner, include it in your literature review and merely accept everything that you have read. You must resist the temptation to adopt the 'sponge approach', that is, soaking everything up and then squeezing it out in the literature review. Instead you need to take a positive approach and to adopt a critical stance by interrogating the literature. You do this by comparing the various pieces of literature you have read, and by asking the sort of questions we identified earlier in the chapter. Remember, you are searching for information that you need to develop your project, which does not mean that you include everything you have read, however great the temptation might be to include it all.

Another useful approach to the literature in order to develop critical analysis is to compare material from a variety of sources. You will be expected to consult articles, books, online materials, official reports and internal documents, and these will be written by a range of authors and interest groups. By comparing the various perspectives you will be able to see if there are differences in the views being put forward. For example, are there significant differences between official publications and research papers? Do policy documents draw on the findings of academic research, and if not why not? Are different authors saying the same thing or are there genuine differences of opinion? The amount of consensus will differ according to your topic, but in the social sciences and humanities there are often differences of opinion between groups and individuals, which, in some cases, can be based on the same research evidence. Developing a thorough understanding of the different perspectives put forward by different authors and sources will enable you to develop a critical overview of the literature and strengthen your final project.

The 'golden rule' is:

> Develop a critical approach in writing your review of the literature.

Looking at literature in chronological order will also enable you to develop a critical approach. You will be able to see how the arguments have changed and developed over a period of time and assess the influence of particular authors. If there is a significant publication that has been the crucial document for your study it will be useful to see how this has been interpreted and used over a period of time. It will also provide a route into a range of other sources as you consider how other writers and policy makers have interpreted and used this document.

It is also important to remember that with some literature you will often only develop a critical approach over a period of time. You are likely to amass a large amount of literature on your topic and as you return to each publication you will develop new ideas and identify different perspectives. You will read material a number of times and discover different aspects that you did not notice initially. As you read more widely you will develop a deeper understanding of your topic area and you will gain greater insight which will enable you to undertake increased critical analysis. Indeed, critical analysis of the literature will also be developed later on in the project as you consider your discussion and conclusion chapters. The literature you have accessed during this initial part of your project will be significant when you come to undertake detailed analysis of your findings later on the project.

 Summary of Chapter Three

This chapter has:

- Considered the purpose of the literature review
- Discussed the overall structure of the review
- Given advice on the different types of literature to use
- Described the use of online materials
- Discussed making use of official publications and reports
- Explored the advantages and disadvantages of using literature from within your own organisation
- Described how you can develop critical analysis.

 **Further reading**

Ridley, D. (2008) *The Literature Review: A Step-by-Step Guide for Students*. London: Sage.

Rumsey, S. (2008) *How to Find Information: A Guide for Researchers*. London: Open University Press.

4

Research Methodology

In Chapter Two, we examined the overall design of the research; we described and explored the main research paradigms; we also looked at case study research. Once you have settled on your research design, having decided which broad approach you are to use, you now have to select the most appropriate method or methods to be used.

In this chapter, the following topics are considered:

- Deciding on the *suitability* of any particular method
- Advantages and disadvantages of the main research instruments – questionnaires, interviews, documentary analysis, observation, diaries and logs
- Issues involved in designing and constructing each of these.

Deciding on the suitability of any particular method

There is a 'golden rule' that can be applied in all cases concerning choice of a research instrument:

Ensure you know what data you wish to collect BEFORE deciding upon the method of collecting it.

It is very tempting to begin the other way round, as we have seen from many examples of students who begin work on, especially their first piece of research, by saying, 'I want to look into X and I think I'll send out a questionnaire to …'! This is entirely the wrong thing to do. By the time you reach your final piece of work, project or dissertation, you should be experienced enough in research to avoid this mistake, but it is well worth emphasising here. You will need to demonstrate to the assessor or examiner that you have thought carefully about the suitability of the instrument(s) selected and used and you can do this by showing that you were clear which data you wanted to collect – and why – and that the instrument was chosen as the best to gather that data. You will of course be using more than one method in your major project, so you need to demonstrate this suitability for each one.

For example, suppose you are researching the effectiveness of departmental team meetings in your own institution, you could at once decide to observe some meetings and examine minutes of the meetings. However, *before* you decide on any such methods, you need to be clear about what you mean by 'effectiveness' and which data will best help you to determine to what extent it exists in the meetings and any records of them. From your reading and literature review, you should be able to devise some criteria for the meetings' effectiveness, which you could set out clearly in a list, such as:

   (i) Clear purpose
   (ii) Agreed agenda
   (iii) Sound timekeeping
   (iv) Opportunity for all attending to contribute
   (v) Definite decisions taken
   (vi) Clarity about follow-up action
   (vii) Fair management/chairing.

Studying your list of criteria, you might decide that data for (iii), (iv) and (vii) could best be found by actually observing the meeting (and, for example, doing the timing yourself!), whereas data for (i) and (ii) could best be found by asking the meeting's participants what they believed the purpose of the meeting was and whether the agenda had been agreed beforehand. This might be done through interviews or questionnaires. Data for (v) and (vi) might be best collected by analysing the subsequent minutes of the meetings. Thus a mixture of research instruments could emerge, containing both quantitative data (such as how much time was spent on each agenda item or topic) and qualitative data (such as the perceptions of attendees as to whether the purpose of the meetings was clear).

Thus, you are able to write about the suitability of the chosen instruments with reference to the specific data that you wanted to collect that would give evidence as to the meeting's effectiveness according to your stated criteria.

So, think carefully about which data will be most helpful to you in helping you to find evidence about the topic you are researching. Consider, for example, the number of times something occurs? Opinions of people concerned? Agreement or disagreement with a statement? And many others. *When* you are clear on the data, then consider which may be the best way to collect that data – that is, the most suitable research instruments.

Choosing the right research instrument

Questionnaires

Surveys using effective questionnaires can reliably find out the perceptions, opinions and attitudes of much larger populations than can be reached by qualitative methods such as interviews. The number of responses enables quantitative data to be gathered and analysed on these opinions or points of view. The aim of a questionnaire is to gather equivalent information from the population concerned and perhaps the crucial thing to remember when designing this particular research instrument is that it 'is in the hands of the respondent, and is completed by him or her' (Johnson, 1994: 37). As Johnson points out, the respondent has choices which include that they 'may complete and return the questionnaire at a time convenient to themselves (i.e. not necessarily convenient to the researcher!), or fail to complete the questionnaire at all' (1994: 37).

The main advantage of a questionnaire is that, if used well, it can elicit information from a far larger number of people than is possible via other methods. Its main disadvantage is that it is difficult to gather in-depth answers to questions and risks being superficial.

There are certain steps to be taken to ensure that your questionnaire is likely to be effective.

It is crucial that you obtain sufficient information about the respondents to your questionnaire to enable you to analyse the data to the best effect for your research. Therefore, the boxes that you place at the beginning of the questionnaire which ask for basic information about the person completing it are crucial. Which boxes you use depends of course upon the exact nature of your research but it is possible that you may wish to know, for example, your respondents':

- Gender
- Status/role/post
- Length of time in post/company
- Length of time in the profession/work
- Qualification(s).

Each or all of these should be formed so that the respondent simply has to tick the relevant box, such as

Male ☐   Female ☐

Role: Director ☐   Manager ☐   Salesperson ☐   Clerical ☐

Years in Post ☐

Years in Company ☐

All this information will help you to sift the replies and classify accordingly (see Chapter Seven). You may argue that you are not interested in researching the gender aspect of your topic. However, it is just possible that the replies from female respondents turn out to be significantly different from those of males, which gives you an extra and interesting dimension to your findings. It may not shed any light at all of course; in which case you have lost nothing by asking for one box to be ticked.

One further point or even warning! Do not ask respondents for their exact age. Most people are offended by this and asking for such information is regarded as intrusive, thus almost guaranteeing non-return of questionnaire. Focus instead on length of experience, as above. However, when age is genuinely important in your research (for example, you could be researching the impact of mature entrants into teaching), use ranges of age:

Age: 20–29 ☐   30–39 ☐   40–49 ☐   50–59 ☐   60+ ☐

Features of a questionnaire likely to attract completion

- It is calculated to take no more than 30 minutes to complete. You are being appreciative of respondents' valuable time.
- The layout is clear and visually appealing.
- It is easy to complete. Use boxes to tick, numbers to circle and similar easy tasks so that most of the respondents' time is spent on thinking, not writing.
- Put the questions in the right order. Put more difficult or sensitive questions later in the questionnaire.
- Try to make the actual wording as precise as possible.
- Avoid giving respondents the chance to 'sit on the fence' in giving their views. For example, use even number scales for rating, do not offer a 'No opinion' box. Note, this is not the same as a 'Don't know' box, which is a perfectly valid choice if questioned about a fact or event.
- Include the all important 'Other(s)' section at the end in case your questions do not cover everything!
- Pilot the questionnaire. (Piloting of all research instruments is addressed in Chapter Five.)

Fowler (2002) adds to such a list by suggesting:

- Use of appropriate incentives
- Reminding respondents several times of the importance of the data
- Personally appealing again to non-respondents, delivering a second questionnaire as necessary.

Fowler (2002) is, of course, partly referring to an accompanying letter issued with the questionnaires, and, if the research is in your own or a nearby institution, contacting via pigeon holes, email and such to remind people of completion dates, the importance of the work and perhaps the incentives!

Finally, Bell (2002: 88) makes the point strongly that 'Respondents have rights'. When someone fails to complete and return your questionnaire s/he is exercising that right so it is your job as the designer and constructor of the instrument to appeal in every professional way possible to their willingness and ability to help.

Some particular things to avoid in questionnaires

- Double questions ('How many seminars do you have in a week and are they useful?')
- Leading questions ('How much of a waste of time are your team meetings?')
- Using a closed question format when you are seeking detail ('Can you remember the first interview you had?')
- Going too far back in time for more experienced respondents ('What was the pass rate for the students in your first year of teaching?')
- Hypothetical questions ('If you had a leader with a different style, would you ...?')
- Questions which assume you already know the respondents' attitudes ('To what extent do you find that an open-door policy is time wasting?')

Using measuring scales in questionnaires

A Likert scale can be used, this will involve respondents in making judgements about the topic being researched. For example, a statement can be made, such as: 'The company's induction programme is helpful to new employees'. Respondents are then asked to respond to the statement by circling the number or ticking a box.

Strongly disagree	Disagree	Agree	Strongly agree
1	2	3	4

You can aggregate the findings by totalling the numbers or ticks to get an overall view of respondents' opinions.

Another scale is one which uses prioritising. You set out certain criteria and ask the respondents to put a number against each one, rating them in order of importance. Make sure you make clear that, for example, 1 equals highest importance and 6 equals lowest importance. For instance, if you were researching issues of job satisfaction in employment, you might say that 'The following seven factors can influence job satisfaction. Please indicate by placing a number against each one the order of importance in *your* personal job satisfaction, where 1 equals the most and 7 equals the least important.

Wages/salary ☐

Prospects of promotion ☐

Relationship with manager ☐

Relationships with work colleagues ☐

The nature of the job itself ☐

Conditions at work (environment, refreshments, hours, etc.) ☐

Company vision/philosophy ☐

Again, by aggregating the numbers you can gain an overall view of what is seen as important or less important across a range of employees.

Summing up, therefore, questionnaires are a widely used method of gaining valuable data from a range of people. To achieve this, the form of the instrument needs to be focused, and attractive to the potential respondent. It should begin in a straightforward questioning way, and all questions should be simple in their structure. The questionnaire is not a suitable instrument for gathering great detail or gaining insight into deep issues which involve potentially complex or emotional reactions. Of course, it *is* possible to gain a general picture of people's emotional responses to, for example, a new pay policy or the redundancies in an organisation. These need to be guided through a scale such as a Likert scale concerning statements about the issue.

	Strongly disagree	Disagree	Agree	Strongly agree
The new pay policy is a de-motivation to experienced employees				
The policy will discourage me from seeking promotion				

OR

Which of the following words most accurately described your feelings when you *first* heard the news about the company's proposals for downsizing?

Disgust ☐   Anger ☐   Fear ☐   Sorrow ☐   Relief ☐

In nearly all cases, details and complexities are best researched through the use of a face-to-face instrument, to which we turn now.

Interviews

As noted by Wragg (2002: 143), 'interviewing is one of the oldest and most widely used of social science research techniques'. It is a very useful technique in researching leadership as it is an inter-personal process, enabling the researcher to engage with leaders and/or 'followers' and delve into some of the aspects which underpin so much of what is involved in leading others. As with all research instruments, interviews of course have a particular focus and purpose.

There are three main types of interview:

- *The structured interview*: This form gives the interviewer very little scope to depart from the set questions. Answers are limited or closed ('yes/no'). Wragg (2002: 149) suggests that 'there is no reason to [do this kind of] interview unless face-to-face questioning really is a superior method'. In other words, use a questionnaire rather than a structured interview, unless there is a compelling reason to put the questions on a face-to-face basis.
- *The unstructured interview*: This type of questioning is to acquire in-depth knowledge and can roam freely over a range of issues. It requires considerable skill and it can be argued that training is needed to handle the process well so that the psychological insights required can be elicited in a sensitive and thorough way.
- *The semi-structured interview*: This is by far the most-used form of interview and we recommend that you use it in your project or dissertation research (when you do use interviewing as an instrument). The semi-structured interview uses a set of carefully devised questions but gives you scope to respond to the interviewee's answer with further option(s) for clarification or emphasis. This means you can adapt to the personality of the interviewee and perhaps any circumstances relating to him/her (e.g. the interviewee arriving late and flustered or having had a stressful day).

In addition to the professionalism, clear-thinking and insight needed for all research instruments, interviewing requires a certain element of social skills in relating to the interviewee who 'may not have previously given deep thought to the issue and may actually be constructing his position during the interview' (Bassey, 1999: 81).

Features of an effective semi-structured interview

- *Location*: Ensure the interview takes place in a comfortable and relaxed environment if possible, and where there will be no interruptions (phone-calls or visitors). The key question, as Wragg (2002: 145) says, as to whether it is office, coffee-lounge, or elsewhere is 'Given the nature of the interview, what location makes most sense?'

- *Time*: As with questionnaires, respect the interviewee's time. Make clear *in advance* how long the interview is likely to take (perhaps 30 minutes is a good average). Keep your eye on the clock and be sensible in politely curtailing rambling answers.
- *Timing*: You will usually of course have to fit in with the interviewee's schedule, as the person is doing you a favour. However, some times of the day will have built-in potential problems that you will need to be aware of. If a Business Manager says 'I can just give you 20 minutes before an important meeting', you may have to seize the opportunity, but be aware that his/her mind may well be on what is going to happen at that meeting. If a class teacher agrees to be interviewed straight after the last lesson of the day, that person may be stressed, with their mind still occupied by an incident that has just occurred. A further factor in timing is to try not to interview too long after something has occurred about which you wish to ask, for example, a new policy coming into force.
- *A clear schedule*: The effective interview will probably have between five and eight questions, with the first one being relatively straightforward and more complex ones coming later. You should prepare the questions carefully and have a series of 'probes' or 'prompts' ready as follow-up questions if the interviewee is too brief in replying or has been evasive or rambling.
- *Recording*: You can either make your own notes or record the interview electronically. You need to ensure that you use the same process for each interview for consistency and you need to obtain in advance the permission of the interviewee for recording electronically. If one interviewee out of six refuses permission for electronic recording you should then take notes for all six interviews. Your data could be challenged if you used different processes to obtain them. Your own preference is important here. Some researchers are comfortable with machines; some have doubts about note taking whilst listening. The important thing about the latter is that only you will read and transcribe the notes, so many research interviewers, unskilled in official shorthand, devise their own codes or versions of shorthand which when they read them later, makes sense to them!

Things to avoid in a semi-structured interview

- Complex questions (see relevant questionnaires section).
- Bringing your own opinion into the interview. You will have your own opinions of course, often strongly held, but you must avoid being drawn into debate. It is the views of the interviewee you are after – you know yours! The interviewee may well say 'Don't you agree?!' or 'I'm sure you agree with that'. Your response

needs to be on the lines of 'I see what you mean', or 'I understand' rather than 'I do so agree!' Retaining your objectivity is crucial.

- Being drawn into discussion which is not relevant to the topic being researched. It could well be something you are very interested in, but if it is not relevant here, politely move on.
- Issues that are too personal and sensitive (see the section on Ethics in Chapter Five for a full discussion of this).
- Letting your feelings about the interviewee influence your response to the answers. You may 'warm' to the person, or you may actually dislike their attitude, but it is what they are *saying* that you record.

One question that practitioner researchers often ask is 'How do you know if the person is telling the truth?' The honest answer is that you cannot be certain, any more than you can be sure that a questionnaire answer is an honest one. Experience helps interviewers to detect through body language, eye avoidance, discomfort or evasiveness, etc. Remember that this is more likely to be because of unease or concern as to whether *you* can be trusted than actual deceit. An isolated case is almost certain to show up in your data analysis.

Skill is also required in being aware of different cultural attitudes towards discussion or questioning. Some cultures have a more deferential attitude than others, so that, for example, appearing to contradict the other person or criticising a work superior would not be acceptable under any circumstances. Other cultures appear more abrupt in language, so that answers which may seem curt and even discourteous to a British person are in fact a normal response. Try to be aware of any potential differences that might exist in preparing for an interview in such circumstances.

Focus group interviews

Sometimes an interview with a small group of, say, four to six people can be very useful. It can be helpful in eliciting data on an issue about which you wish to gain a representative view, or a general feeling about a topic indicative of the life of the institution. It can be particularly helpful in getting data from children or students, where the population is very large and where individuals might lack confidence or feel intimidated in a one-to-one interview.

In focus group interviews, you act as much as a facilitator as questioner, remembering to listen most of the time. Beware of one or two individuals dominating proceedings but when one person corrects or amends what another has said, use that to intervene, and see if a consensus arises. If you are taking notes, do not forget to note who is who, probably on a simple diagram, to aid your recording. If you are recording electronically, you may need them to each state their first names each time they speak.

Telephone and online interviewing

Sometimes, circumstances arise which mean it is not practicable to carry out a face-to-face interview and it becomes necessary to do a telephone interview. Here, it is crucial to follow the same procedures as in face-to-face. The same schedule should be used and, if possible, the same approaches in terms of staying relevant, using tact to curtail over-long answers and asking the interviewee to clarify or repeat if the answer is unclear.

The use of the internet is developing in research, with discussion groups, visual diaries, blogs, all beginning to be used. However, it is not recommended to practitioner researchers as an interview instrument because it immediately becomes a 'written document' and is therefore placed in a different category altogether.

Observation

Whole books have been written about observational processes, so it is important to recognise in terms of your purposes in carrying out your research some key issues involved in using it.

Observation can be complex and difficult because of the nature of having to watch so many things happening at the same time. It therefore requires very careful preparation. It can also be very time-consuming. It is very unlikely that you will have time to do the kind of research which enables you to mingle with office, work or school life and observe in a naturalistic way (participant observation). However, observing management meetings or a leader throughout a day ('shadowing') both require plenty of your time and the arrangements for timings are not under your control; for example, you have to observe a meeting when it is scheduled to take place.

Because of the issue in observation of many things occurring at the same time, it is more important than ever with this instrument that the following 'golden rule' is remembered:

Observation needs to have a clear formulated purpose and focus.

You are most likely to use *structured* observation for your research and operate on a *non-participant* basis. The key questions are:

- What is to be observed?
- How should observations be recorded?

Formal or relatively structured gatherings of people are much easier for the practitioner researcher to observe than informal work settings such as the staff restaurant. It is sensible to focus on a formal meeting (even though it may be relatively informal!), or a discussion group, or the movements of an individual leader or manager ('shadowing'). In observing these you will need to be selective and therefore clear about precisely what you are going to observe and record at, say, a formal meeting. What you choose to observe must be likely to give you data about the topic you are researching. For example, you could be researching the actual quality of meetings (see earlier) *or* you could be researching organisational culture, and therefore observing meetings as an indicator of the type of culture.

You may choose to record by, for example, a video-recording of a meeting, where you may not yourself even be present. Whether you record in this way or by operating as a 'fly on the wall', marking your devised observation schedule, there is always one issue that needs to be noted, that is, whether the participants are performing as normally as they would if no observer were present.

It is often said about any kind of observation that as soon as a 'third party' enters the situation, that situation becomes an artificial one. In schools or colleges, observation is regularly carried out in classrooms (for example, for recruitment purposes, during periods of training, or for performance appraisal) and the more regularly it is done, the less artificial it may become. However it cannot be denied that it is 'not normal' and the research observer needs simply to follow all the professional and courteous procedures to make the situation as near to normal as possible. The overriding principle in observation is that the observers draw as little attention to themselves as possible.

It can be argued that this reservation about artificiality is no different from knowing whether someone is telling the truth at an interview. You simply need to be aware of this issue. There is some evidence that, if the observers are genuinely 'obscure', people quickly forget their presence (or the camera's) and get on with normal behaviour. This situation can be exacerbated if you as observer are personally known to the participants (see Chapter Six on 'Practitioner Research').

Case example 4.1

Sheila's final project for her Masters in Business Studies was focused on HRM and she was researching the leadership styles operating within a specific business organisation. She decided, as one of her instruments, to carry out structured

(Continued)

(Continued)

observations of a number of meetings. These were chaired by a Senior Manager and described in the firm's recruitment literature as 'enabling staff to contribute ideas to the firm's development and encourage a spirit of mutual openness'. Based on a good deal of her reading of Williams (1994), Sheila devised an observation schedule, which involved a simple diagram and an accompanying chart. On the diagram, she noted:

- The number of times each attendee spoke to the chair
- Whether this was a reactive or proactive comment
- The number of times an individual spoke to another (not the chair). By drawing arrows, she was able to record exactly who spoke to whom and how often.

On the accompanying chart, she noted key words which occurred frequently, recording each time the word was used and who used it. Through this chart, she hoped to discern whether there were patterns or themes to be elicited.

The data from the observations enabled her to consider issues such as the extent to which:

- The chair dominated the meeting – procedure and content
- Each attendee contributed
- Dialogue not via the chair occurred
- Talk was initiated by the chair and by others.

Plus:

- The extent to which there was a common vocabulary
- The extent to which individuals followed the chair's words or the words of others
- Whether individuals used different words from others.

The data from three separate meetings proved illuminating for Sheila's analysis and, when triangulated with her documentary analysis data, gave insights into the meetings as an indicator of leadership approaches in the organisation.

Shadowing and task observation

Both these forms of observation normally relate to researching the nature of a person's work. Shadowing, which we briefly referred to above, describes the process in which the researcher follows the person being observed through an agreed period, noting all the activities and processes that occur. It is particularly helpful in trying to capture the essence of a 'typical' day in work. Unlike the example given (Case Example 4.2) where the working person makes his/her own record of activities, shadowing involves the observer doing the recording, leaving the observed free to go about their customary business. A few points that are similar to the use of other instruments should be noted:

- Shadowing can be time-consuming.
- The best form of sheet for recording is a time-based one with a note being made of what occurred at each particular time. The analysis into categories will come afterwards.
- The behaviour of the observed may have an element of artificiality, as noted with other observations. For example, the language used in a manager repri-manding someone may be influenced by the knowledge that someone else is present. Again, although it is more difficult here, make yourself as observer as unobtrusive as possible.
- The question of what is a 'typical' day again arises and here you are likely to have to accept the day chosen by your subject.

Task observation is where the researcher observes someone carrying out a specified task. It has been used as part of a performance review. Thus what is observed is a single task or process, not a general view of work or a series of interaction. Examples might include observing the subject carrying out an interview or conducting a school assembly. Again, preparation should include having a schedule or time chart or a set of criteria to tick off when something meeting that criteria is observed.

Use of diaries, time logs and reflective logs

Morrison (2002: 213) describes diary-focused research as 'a distinctive genre that straddles both quantitative and qualitative approaches'. She points out that: 'Diary keepers are either researchers or research participants or both' (2002: 213). We are here dealing with the situation where the researcher com-missions others to complete a particular schedule devised by the researcher over a fixed period of time, enabling the researcher to have data for analysis at the end of that period. The data produced are obviously particularly useful in reviewing certain processes at work, or providing evidence for the nature of a specific role. These schedules may be in the form of:

- A log book in which the participant records comments/reflections on, for exam-ple, the day's incidents, or specified emotions
- A time chart in which the participant marks at specific periods under specific headings what has occurred (see Figure 4.1 for an example)
- A 'critical incident' diary in which particular incidents (previously defined) are noted and commented on as they occur.

	9.30–10.00	10.00–10.30	10.30–11.00	11.00–11.30	11.30–12.00	12.00–12.30	12.30–1.00	1.00–1.30	1.30–2.00	2.00–2.30	2.30–3.00	etc.
Monday (date)												
Tuesday (date)												
Wednesday (date)												

Activities Key:

Scheduled meetings = M

Spontaneous meetings = S

Discussions with colleagues = C

Meeting clients at base = MB

Telephone/email = TEM

Documents work = D

Visits to clients = V

Other = O

Please place the appropriate symbol in the time space provided. If more than one occurs in that time, please put 2 (or more) symbols.

Figure 4.1 Time log for research respondent to keep

This particular instrument can offer fascinating insights into the reality of people's actual lives at work and the nature of the work itself. However, it has one potential disadvantage that needs careful consideration at the outset.

Completion is in the hands of the participants, and, whilst this is also true of questionnaires, here you are asking a great deal more from them as you are asking them to remember to complete the log regularly over a period of time, and they will usually be busy, working professionals.

Obviously, choosing the people that you ask to keep the diary or chart becomes crucially important. They not only have to be people who 'fit the bill' in terms of what you are researching, but they have to be committed to doing the task – and likely to remember. Incentives could be important here! In our Case Example 4.2, Max used bottles of wine and/or chocolates!

A special value of journals or diaries is that they can provide a very personal and human insight into the process being researched. They offer a reflective way for the person completing the record to view an incident which, on analysis, can provide data both about the actual incident and also the person. Journals or diaries often provide illustrative anecdotes which can so often bring an otherwise rather dry record to life and these can be invaluable to the researcher when writing the final report (see Chapter Nine). The less positive side is that there may be a good deal of data to be sifted out, and selecting what is crucial and relevant to your research topic becomes an all-important task for the researcher in analysing the data. Also, the guidelines given to those willing to complete them will necessarily be relatively broad, and what one person sees as an important incident may be seen by another as normal or even trivial.

 Case example 4.2

Max was a Head of Year (HOY) in a secondary school and wanted to research for his Masters dissertation the role of Heads of Year and, since the literature suggested the risk of many HOYs being more 'trouble shooters' than pastoral and curriculum managers, he decided to investigate what six HOYs in different schools actually spent their time on in carrying out their jobs. Having selected and got the agreement of six such people (the incentives *were* important!), he devised a time chart which involved them merely putting a tick in various blocks of time. He chose 20-minute blocks because each lesson of the day was in

(Continued)

(Continued)

units of an hour, morning break was 20 minutes and lunch was 40 minutes. From his reading he selected several relatively broad headings such as: dealing with parents; student behaviour; discussion with staff; meetings; admin; teaching; assessing work; plus 'other' (!) and the participant ticked the most appropriate box for each block of time. They could tick more than one if they had, for example, seen both a parent and a colleague in the same block. He left a *brief* space for comments daily. Since the notion was to capture the essence of a typical HOY's day, they were asked to ignore training days, examination days or whole days out of school. Rather than expect them to remember every day for a whole week, Max asked them to complete a Monday, Wednesday and Friday in Week One, plus Tuesday and Thursday the next week. They were then asked to leave the task for two weeks and repeat the process again – twice. He thought this structure would give sufficient 'randomness' to capture the variety of tasks involved, plus prove less onerous on the participants. Five of the six completed the task, with one defaulting after two weeks.

The data generated by Max's time charts were considerable and extremely varied. However, he was able to do a good deal of quantitative analysis, examining the percentage of time HOYs spent on student behaviour or seeing parents or on each of the other categories. There were also several in the 'Other' category, including 'dealing with an intruder'!

When these data were triangulated with data from two other instruments (semi-structured interviews and analysis of HOY job descriptions), an illuminating picture emerged of the reality of life for these particular school managers, enabling debate to ensue which could examine and improve the role's effectiveness.

Documentary analysis

Documents are mostly of great value to the researcher and the analysis of selected documents as a research instrument has some significant advantages:

- It is mostly 'desk-top' research. You do not have to visit for an interview or arrange and carry out an observation. Once the documents are collected, you can sit at your desk and peruse and annotate in your own time frame.
- It is low cost. There is likely to be very little postage (if any) involved and few travel costs. Documents can be collected when you 'happen to visit' a school or business; it is even possible to ask a colleague or friend to collect some for you. Furthermore, all educational documents are public ones and therefore free and most companies are happy to provide their 'normal' documents to you. Many documents can be downloaded from the internet free of charge.

- The documents exist independently of the researcher and can sometimes be used as they are opportunistically found. Documents can give the history of an event or process which can provide an important context for what is being researched now.
- They are particularly valuable for providing important other viewpoints than those gained through interview, questionnaire, or other research instruments. They are therefore very useful for purposes of triangulation (see Chapter Five). Examples of this are discussed later in this chapter.

However, there are some potential limitations, such as:

- Documents may include accounts which are biased or provide only a single perspective.
- The document and its data were not compiled specifically for the purpose for which you use it.
- You may not acquire a complete set of certain documents.
- Not all the contents of some documents may be available to you because of their personal or sensitive nature.

What can be seen as documents for research analysis?

The list is considerable: policies, plans, strategy documents, marketing material, brochures, staff recruitment papers including advertisements, official statistics, annual statements, departmental or whole institution handbooks, newsletters, meeting minutes, external (e.g. inspection) reports, memoranda, notice board material, and increasingly, information found on websites and emails.

It is not likely, although not impossible, that you will base the research for your final project primarily on document analysis, but it is an extremely valuable instrument to provide triangulation with other instruments, as the Case Examples 4.1 and 4.2 (above). In terms of carrying out the actual analysis of documents, the following questions will be helpful for you to address:

- What is the purpose of the document?
- What is the context of the document?
- What readership is the document intended for?
- How objective – or subjective – is the tone of the document?
- What kind of language is used?
- Do the illustrations, if any, complement the words?
- Does the layout have any special features?
- Is the document representative – typical or untypical?
- Is the document genuine or has it been 'censored' in some way?

(See Scott (1990) for some criteria concerning documents which are records.)

Some of these questions will be more important than others, depending upon the focus of your research. Sometimes, a content analysis, looking at key words (as in the observation described earlier in Case Example 4.1) can be very helpful in terms of assessing a document's context, readership and purpose.

If we look at the first of our Case Examples (4.1), you recall that Sheila used structured observation to obtain data about meetings in the organisation. She then used documentary analysis of the minutes of these meetings to triangulate that data. She was afterwards able to compare the two sets of data obtained. Some of the above questions were extremely relevant to her analysis. She wanted to know, for example:

- Who wrote the minutes?/Who checked them?/Were they edited?
- Was the tone objective, recording what was said?
- Did the sets of minutes follow a common format?
- Were points for action recorded and who was to act?

By analysing the minutes each time, Sheila was also able to note at the next observation whether the minutes were challenged or amended, and whether the actions noted to be carried out had been done and whether this was reported.

The conclusions coming from Sheila's data analysis throw interesting light upon the organisation's claim that the meetings represented an 'opportunity to contribute' to development and a culture of 'mutual openness'. With that analysis and semi-structured interviews with a senior manager and five attendees at meetings, she was able to make recommendations about operating the meetings in a way which more accurately reflected the organisation's aims.

In Case Example 4.2, Max's analysis of the official HOY job descriptions in each school showed, when compared with the data collected through his time charts, that the 'Other tasks as required by the School Leadership' constituted a huge proportion of what people in the role actually did! Other tasks involving 'curriculum management' were barely present in the reality of the job. Max's own school responded to his research with a revision of the job description and a partial re-structuring of the pastoral system.

Using elements of both quantitative and qualitative research can be very useful in ensuring the idea of triangulation. 'Mixed Methods Research' has a whole journal devoted to its application, although Giddings (2006: 195) has warned that certain 'pressures may lead to demands for the quick fix that mixed methods appears to offer'.

Triangulation is dealt with in Chapter Five and Giddings's warning needs to be considered both in planning your research (Chapters One and Two) and in your Conclusion (Chapter Seven).

Summary of Chapter Four

This chapter has:

- Described how to assess the suitability of your chosen research instruments to the research topic
- Described the features of effective questionnaires and interviews and the pitfalls to avoid in constructing them
- Given practical advice, with practitioner case examples, on carrying out effective observations, documentary analysis and the use of diaries or logs
- Commented briefly on the mixed methods approach to research.

Further reading

Coleman, M. and Briggs, A. (2002) *Research Methods in Educational Leadership and Management*. London: Sage.

Creswell, J. (2002) *Research Design: Qualitative, Quantitative and Mixed Methods Approaches*, 2nd edn. Thousand Oaks, CA: Sage.

5

Applying Research Methods

In this chapter we deal with the various principles and processes that need to be applied in using the research methods described in the previous chapter. Therefore the following issues are considered:

- Piloting or trialling your selected research instrument(s)
- Deciding upon the sample for their use
- Using triangulation and ensuring validity and reliability
- Following the appropriate ethical procedures in research
- The use of specific research literature
- Setting out the Methodology section of your project or dissertation.

Piloting your research instrument(s)

Whichever form of research instrument you have selected as the most appropriate for your specific topic, it is crucial that you ensure that in its final form, it is as focused and accurate as possible for its purpose, that of giving you the data you need. Any errors or ambiguities can have a disastrous effect on the data and also on the completion and response rate. Some respondents will reject a questionnaire, for example, if it has errors or is unclear. 'If they can't be bothered to get it right ...', says the person asked to complete it and the bin is the usual place for it then!

To avoid any such problems, it is important that you pilot your instrument with a view to having any errors discovered, and the instrument corrected and improved. Above all, piloting an instrument brings an objective view to it. As with proof-reading your own material, for example, the creator sees what s/he wants to see and when we construct a questionnaire or an observation schedule, we ourselves understand precisely what we mean!

What do we mean by piloting?

Piloting is also sometimes called 'trialling' or 'practising' in some literature. It refers to the process of trying out your selected research instrument prior to using it in the actual research, for the reasons just mentioned. Some of the questions to be considered before piloting include:

- With whom should it be piloted?
- How many people should be used?
- How many times should it be piloted?

We will consider this in relation to each instrument in turn.

Piloting questionnaires

Ideally you should try to find a small group of people similar to the population you intend for your research and pilot the questionnaire. For example, if you are planning to send a questionnaire to all the administrative and clerical staff in companies in a specific geographical area, try to find a few such people (three to five is sufficient) in a different area who will be willing to spend a few minutes completing the questionnaire for you. Give them the same instructions as in your proposed model, but tell them if they do not understand or cannot answer any questions to say so, and mark the questionnaire accordingly. If a question does not seem relevant, ask them to say so. Unlike some actual research, it is quite acceptable to use personal contacts for piloting, as long as you have not discussed in detail the questionnaire's purposes. So, if you have friends or colleagues, or their partners, who fit the bill, use them. They are usually honest enough to say 'I don't know what you were getting at there' or 'It made no sense to me'.

Those of you in a group studying for a Masters or similar qualification are often able to use other members of the group to pilot (again, as long as you have not discussed details). These are favours you can do for each other.

When the piloted questionnaires have been returned, you will need to study them to see which questions were seen as unclear, and for what reason. Were the questions badly worded? Did they draw a blank from all pilot respondents?

However, in analysing and where necessary amending the returned pilot questionnaires, Bell (2002: 167) reminds us that there is another very important reason for piloting a questionnaire and that is that the returns will help you to consider 'how you will record and analyse your returns: when the "real" questionnaires are returned, you need to know what to do with them'.

So, in some cases the questions may have been clear and understood but did the pilot answers give you information in a way that can be recorded easily, accumulated and give you meaningful data for analysis? If simple distribution or frequency records are required, all well and good for some answers but more complex analysis is likely to be needed in some places. Did the questions which asked for more detailed answers, such as a sentence or two, give answers which lend themselves to analysis, for example? Each time you look at a pilot answer, consider two points:

- Was the question clear and unambiguous?
- Will the answer lend itself to helpful recording and analysis?

Of course, life is never simple and in your pilot returns, you may well find that one question is answered satisfactorily by some and the same question is queried as vague by others. As it is a trial exercise, you have to consider *all* comments and it is likely that if a single person is unclear, the wording of the question is worth re-considering. You may conclude that the question is fine and of course even some of the final actual returns may be faulty, but at least the exercise has forced you to look at the instrument again, through the eyes of another person.

If the pilot returns showed only a few or very minor amendments to be necessary, you can make these and feel satisfied that the final questionnaire is now ready for use. If there were many problems, you may have to consider a second pilot. Although this is time-consuming, it is better than risking a poor questionnaire! Should this be necessary, perhaps piloting it with just two or three people will be sufficient.

All of the above process should have made you aware that you need to allow plenty of time for piloting your questionnaire when you plan the schedule for your project or dissertation. Build the sending out, receiving and amending of the pilot into your timetable – otherwise you risk problems.

Finally, record carefully the changes you make to the original questionnaire, keeping copies, because you will need to report your piloting in the writing up of your methodology for your project or dissertation.

Piloting interviews

When you have constructed your interview schedule, with its list of questions and prompts, it is important that you try it out with one or two typical respondents. As with questionnaires, you can modify the questions afterwards in the light of responses. Unlike questionnaires, it is sometimes possible to modify an interview schedule *during* the actual pilot interview. If, for example, you realised after an early question that your question was insufficiently non-directive, you could amend later questions in the light of this. For example, in interviewing about the quality of training: 'Tell me about the recent training course you attended' is much more open than: 'What problems did you have on the recent training course?' With interviews, the scrutiny of pilot answers is particularly important in considering how the answers will lend themselves to analysis as their data are less easy than questionnaire data to present (see Chapter Seven). Again, record the changes you make to the interview schedule and keep copies, so that you can report this in your writing up.

Piloting observations

This could be very time-consuming and also requires some tact and diplomacy! If your actual research is going to include observing a meeting, for example, the best approach to arranging a pilot of your observation schedule is to ask someone you know if you could 'sit in' on a meeting – or probably just part of it – to trial your schedule, as you need to see if it works. Everyone at the meeting needs to know why you are there, that you are not using their names and that you are merely recording certain interactions on a sheet – you are not really interested in what the meeting is about.

At the pilot observation, mark your schedule carefully – you will fairly quickly find out if it is working or not. Leave the meeting, analyse whether the recording will give you data on what you are trying to find out about, and modify accordingly.

Piloting diaries or time logs

Piloting these research instruments is probably easier than those already mentioned but it is still important to try out any form of time chart before its actual research use. In a case such as that of Max in Chapter Four (Case Example 4.2) who wanted to research what a typical Head of Year did during the working day, the obvious thing to do is to ask a Head of Year in your own school to use it. Just trying to record what is required for a day or two will soon show the user whether it is practicable or not, whether the headings are helpful, whether the blocks of time are too short or too long. Following this feedback, amendments can be made and the new instrument tried again, perhaps just for a day. Although Max was himself a Head of Year and had naturally used his own daily experiences to help devise the headings, it was still important to get one other colleague to pilot the chart in order to bring the necessary objectivity to the exercise. Yet again, note amendments made and keep for reference, ready for the final report writing up.

Piloting documentary analysis

This particular instrument cannot really be piloted in the normal sense, but it is important to *practise* the kind of analysis you plan to use on a similar document. For example, if you intend analysing company recruitment literature, find a sample document and apply some of the criteria described in Chapter Four. Here, you will be looking to see whether the data this produces can give you anything meaningful for your actual analysis.

One point is worth adding about piloting: IF the questionnaire (or interview) is completely unaltered after the pilot and IF those who did the pilot were wholly representative of the sample you applied the actual instrument to, it is possible to add the pilot responses to the total responses you obtain. However, the two conditions just stated must apply for this to be done.

Deciding your sample

Having conducted your instrument in a form with which you are satisfied, the next key questions are: with whom do you use it and how many? From the population that you intend to deal with in your research, the decisions to be made are therefore:

- Which type of sample should be used?
- What size should the sample be?

These two questions should be addressed in that order, so that a 'golden rule' to remember is:

> Decide first on *which* people and *then* on how many.

As you will be hoping to be able to generalise from your findings from a survey, for example, the sample of people you choose should broadly be representative of your population so that your generalisation will be valid. It is important to know of the various types of sampling, some of which you are more likely than others to use for your project research. We focus here on the main types for your use.

Types of sampling

- *Random sampling*: This is where you take the whole list of people available to you (your population) and select your sample on the basis which means those chosen simply 'happen to come out of the hat', such as choosing every fifth name on the list, a common device in random sampling. Of course the size of the sample needs to be decided at this stage (discussed below). You need to consider ways in which any list of people may be constructed in considering whether to use a random sample of every fourth or fifth name. For example, a full staff list of an organisation might be a list of people in alphabetical order of surname which could work well. However, the list might be hierarchical with executives at the head and so on through to ground floor staff. Choosing every fourth name would not necessarily give you the representative sample you seek. A class register in a school might list boys and girls separately and you would need to check numbers to see if random sampling would give you the representative proportion of male and female which is accurate.
- *Stratified sampling*: This is when you wish to ensure that your sample contains sufficient members of particular groups to give you data relevant to your research. Thus you might divide the population by gender, or roles, to ensure that you are sampling sufficient people in a particular category to give your findings validity. Thus, if we wish to obtain the views of marketing managers via a questionnaire, or primary school subject leaders, the sample will be devised accordingly. Sometimes, in researching specialist or minority areas, we need to ensure the sample contains different proportions to what would be found in the whole population. Fogelman (2002: 100) gives a clear example of this:

> ... if we wished to compare the experiences of children with a relatively rare disability with those in the general population of children, then we would probably need to use different sampling fractions for the two groups. In this way, we could ensure the minority group is large enough within our sample to make that analysis possible.

The above two types of sampling are known as probability sampling, along with others you may encounter such as cluster sampling. Under non-probability sampling there are three types which you may find useful.

- *Convenience sampling*: Sometimes known as opportunity sampling, this is often used by practitioners in their research because practitioners who are in full employment while they do the research have much less time than paid higher education researchers and find anything helpful which appears to save time, as the term 'convenience' suggests. This sample is one which is chosen because it is available to the researcher, obvious examples being the company, school, office or college where the researcher works. This sampling can be valid but needs to be carefully checked (how will it affect the conclusions to be drawn?), and of course explained in the writing up.

An example of working professionals using this approach that we have seen is in attending a training course for specific groups of people in particular roles. Sarah, a head of Physical Education (PE) in a secondary school, had constructed a questionnaire for heads of PE Departments in a Local Authority (LA) region. Each term, all these heads of departments were invited to a regional conference for a day which included a good deal of group discussion work. Sarah took copies of her questionnaire into the conference and gave them to the attendees to take away and complete. She felt that she: (a) saved half the postage money! and (b) made them more likely to complete as she had asked them personally.

Of course, the timing of such a meeting has to be appropriate to fit in with the research schedule, and not everyone would attend the conference. However, questionnaires could be posted to absentees to ensure 100% coverage.

Such an approach can be particularly helpful in selecting a sample for your interviews, as, again, a personal request can be very persuasive compared with a letter or email.

- *Purposive sampling*: This is where the researcher specifically selects the sample because (s)he uses judgement or experience to assess their representativeness. 'I know just the person', 'She would be ideal' would be the reactions in this case. This sampling is appropriate, especially for interview samples, as long as you carefully justify your reasons for selecting the person when you are writing up. For example, if you wanted to sample marketing managers about government guidelines for advertising procedures and you knew someone who had been involved in an area consultative working party, you might decide to interview that particular person, knowing she would have good knowledge of how the guidelines were devised.
- *Snowball sampling*: This is usually used when potential people are difficult to find. So, to use the example above, if you were researching how advertising guidelines were devised, you might interview the person described above and then ask them if they could identify or recommend someone else you could interview, then repeat the process, and so on.

Size of sample

There can be no hard and fast rule about the size of a sample, that is, how many respondents should be approached to make the research results meaningful. There are perhaps two guiding principles we can mention:

- Practicability
- Validity.

First, the practical aspects of research, especially for practitioners, are important, particularly in terms of time and expense. It might ideally be desirable to survey by questionnaire a thousand people but the expense would be prohibitive. And do you really have the time to organise all those contact details? While size is important, '... of at least equal importance is the way the sample is drawn. A small probability sample free of bias is preferable to a large sample that is biased and unrepresentative ...' (Fogelman, 2002: 103).

In general, it may be said that the larger the sample for a survey, the more likely we are to have results from which we can generalise with reasonable confidence. There is no magic number. In certain kinds of qualitative research not involving surveys, an in-depth study of a few individuals can be sufficient and produce insightful results. You will read articles where researchers have had a sample of just five or six interviewees (e.g. headteachers, or company directors) and have drawn meaningful data from these, supported by a literature review.

For your purposes, in general terms, a minimum of 30 respondents might be a useful guide for a questionnaire. Of course, what we have described and discussed above are the samples which are planned for, especially in questionnaires or interviews. However, it is virtually certain that you will not receive 100% responses to what you send out – this is extremely rare. Therefore, you also need to consider the *actual sample* based on responses. This is particularly important if there is a risk that the number of those returning the questionnaire is so small that the sample cannot be seen as representative. Additionally, there is a risk of those small numbers returning the questionnaire forming a relatively biased sub-group of the intended sample. Imagine, for example, you send out 70 questionnaires which ask whether the respondents are in favour of or against a particular policy. If you receive, say, only 20 replies and of those 17 are against the policy, you would be foolish to conclude that the population you were targeting was on the whole 'anti-policy'. On a larger return of, say, 50 out of 70, those 17 might be virtually the only ones against. Perhaps they felt more strongly about the policy and so returned the forms? It is impossible to be sure.

Thus the number for your sample should allow for some non-response. Two-thirds or more is generally seen as an acceptable rate of response to a postal survey, so you can use that in calculating the size of your sample.

Case example 5.1

George, a primary school teacher in the East Midlands in England, wanted to research the impact of School Improvement Teams (SITs) in a Local Authority geographical area upon the school's development over a recent three-year

(Continued)

(Continued)

period. These SITs were small voluntary groups of staff in each school. What contribution had these made to school improvement since their inception? How had they operated?

He decided to survey a sample of staff who were not SIT members in all five schools concerned and interview one member of each SIT from each school. The total population of staff across the five schools was 172. Taking out SIT members, this was reduced to 146. He also decided to omit the five headteachers, leaving 141. Initially, George opted for a random sample of 70, every other name on the staff list. However, there were complications! George reasoned that only those staff who had been at the school for at least two years could reasonably comment on improvement. This omission of relatively new staff skewed the sample at the largest school, where many new teachers had been appointed when a new head arrived the previous year. A further problem was the balance between teaching and assistant staff in some schools. In one set of returns, a scrutiny of the respondents' boxes showed that only two teachers had returned the question-naire whilst nine assistant staff had, which was quite disproportionate to the normal teacher–assistant ratio.

Although he had successfully piloted his questionnaire and interview schedule in a parallel school elsewhere, the response analysis left George with a seriously distorted sample. He had wanted to be inclusive and gain the views of all staff, but now felt this had backfired on him. He should, he realised, have used a stratified sample, ensuring representative numbers from both teaching and assistant staff in the appropriate proportions. The data he obtained could not be claimed to be representative of *staff* views, and he had to try again!

Ensuring your research is valid

When the research has been carried out, results produced and conclusions drawn, basic questions will be asked. Easterby-Smith et al. (2002: 89) put these bluntly: 'will the research stand up to outside scrutiny and will anyone believe what I am saying about it?'

For the answers to these questions to be positive, it is essential to ensure that you have done all you can to ensure that your research has been as valid and reliable as possible. There are a cluster of words found in the literature which may be used here, such as:

- Reliability
- Validity
- Generalisability

- Credibility
- Authenticity.

This number of different terms can be confusing to a Masters student. Here we try to stress the need to make the research as unproblematic as possible and to clarify terms. The first issue to mention is the process of triangulation.

- *Triangulation* – is the 'back-and-forth comparison of data from different sources' (James et al., 2008: 60), and is where a variety of research methods are used to compare sources of data relating to the specific research question. This process helps to make the results of research more meaningful, since they do not rely on any one particular method of enquiry. This is especially effective in the Social Sciences field because the different aspects of human behaviour can be studied from more than one perspective. Bush (2002: 68) reminds us, however, that triangulation is also occurring when a variety of respondents are being questioned about a particular issue. In dissertations or projects at Masters level, it is common for both kinds of triangulation to be used. For example, a questionnaire could be sent to teachers in a school, or employees in an office, interviews carried out with parents, or with a firm's clients and observation done of pupils, or management meetings. This kind of approach attempts to give as many different viewpoints as possible on the central topic being researched. Each method and each respondent gives an opportunity for cross-checking the data gathered from any particular source. It is important to apply the principles of proper sampling, discussed above, in each separate method and set of respondents, however; any haste to have a variety of methods and/ or respondents must not dilute the quality of the researchers' work. A 'triangulation matrix' is sometimes referred to in the literature, but we have known students who have successfully used a form of triangulation chart which can provide a very useful summary for all researchers, by helping them keep their focus on the actual questions, reminding them precisely what it is they are seeking from each respondent group. See Figure 5.1.
- *Validity* – can be seen as 'whether research accurately describes the phenomenon which it is intended to describe' (Bush, 2002: 65). Herr and Anderson (2005) propose various types of validity, such as:

  o Outcome validity – where the result of the research proved effective
  o Dialogic validity – where a diverse group of respondents can be seen to have participated in the process
  o Democratic validity – where those normally less represented are seen to have participated in the process and contributed to the results.

These however are likely to be much less important to the assessor than the validity which deals with the accuracy and objectivity of your research process. Issues of how to recognise the significance of non-response to questionnaires or avoiding bias in interviews have already been discussed.

Bush (2002: 67) links the notion of external validity with the *generalisability* of the findings: that is, can the findings from this research be transferred to other settings or locations? We have noted above the use of a number of such words in the literature on research and you will encounter writers who dispute some of the terms as having real meaning. Our advice is to be clear about *your* understanding of say, 'validity', and note that 'generalisability' may be listed quite separately. The crucial thing in your own work is that you are consistent in your use of the word as far as its meaning and application are concerned. For example, you could apply 'validity' to your process and 'generalisability' to your findings.

- *Reliability* – there is general agreement that reliability refers to the fact that if you repeated the procedures of research, similar results would be obtained, thus 'It provides a degree of confidence that replicating the process would ensure consistency' (Bush, 2002: 60). Reliability therefore asks:

   o Whether the findings of the population questioned accurately represent the entire population of which they are part? (Is your sample reliable?)
   o Whether the duplication of the research process produces similar results? (Are your methods reliable?)

And Lewis and Ritchie (2003) add a third:

   o Whether the findings provoke greater ideas about the larger field of study of which they are a part? (You would normally address this in your conclusions about your findings, relating them back to the 'big picture' of your literature review.)

Some research writers (e.g. James et al., 2008) refer to the notion of credibility, used in the common-sense meaning of whether your conclusions make sense. However, this is, as acknowledged, a subjective judgement and our advice about these terms in a technical sense is as given above, stressing again the need for consistency in your use of them.

The final point to be made is that it is crucial that you yourself recognise and acknowledge overtly any imperfections in your research. There is no such thing as the perfect piece of research! Questions that you realise afterwards should have been asked but were not could have affected your data. You get full credit for acknowledging this in your writing up. You may have become aware of a flaw in your sample or piloting, in which case you need to state your awareness of this. We address this both in Chapter Nine on Writing Up and in Chapter Ten on Assessment. All this is clear evidence that you have learned about the research process whilst carrying out your project.

Following the appropriate ethical procedures

For all sorts of very sound reasons, there is today a strong emphasis on ethics in research. All of us have become aware of cheating and misrepresentation,

Research question	Respondents (number)	Instrument	Data sought

When the data have been received, the chart can still be used to record the usefulness of the information in each column, checking it against other data.

Figure 5.1   A simple triangulation chart

even ill treatment, in highly publicised cases in medical science in the fairly recent past which have further prompted all those involved in research of any kind to ensure clear ethical procedures are followed. All HE institutions have strict procedures and protocols for both staff and students. Your own institution will almost certainly require you to complete some kind of ethical approval form, so that your research can be checked in advance that it is adhering to the ethical standards expected. (See Chapter Six for an example of an ethical approval form.)

As Busher (2002: 75) notes, the context for ethical standards is constantly changing, '... ethical principles and moral guidelines have to be located within their contemporary and historical, political, social, cultural and epistemological frameworks'. No doubt your own context will change over the years ahead. In the twenty-first century, the great stress on the rights of the individual place greater emphasis on the researcher respecting those rights. Such legislation affecting qualitative researchers in Britain as, for example, the Human Rights Act, the Data Protection Act and the Freedom of Information Act, all remind researchers of the need to ensure the rights of *all* those involved are respected. In some countries every person and/or institution involved in research is required to give *written* permission for the research to be carried out. You will need to know your own institution's regulations concerning this, and adhere to them accordingly. Even without legislation and bureaucratic demands, contexts change rapidly, bringing new potential dilemmas. New technology is an obvious example – how can you preserve anonymity in a videoed observation, for example? With the availability of so much data on the internet, how can files be kept confidential? We cannot provide answers to all dilemmas, but we will explain the standards expected and describe where in the stages of research you need to be vigilant that you follow ethical procedures.

The first point to remember is that appropriate procedures have to be followed at *all* stages of the research. In the literature review (Chapter Three) avoiding plagiarism is obviously a key ethical standard. In the data analysis (Chapter Seven) any deliberate misrepresentation of the data is an equally serious matter.

Underpinning your ethical approach to your research is the acknowledgement that participation by others is *voluntary* and no one can or should be pressured or coerced. Therefore participants' consent is needed and this is normally known as 'informed consent', that is, people know what it is they are agreeing to take part in. This issue in ethics in research embodies the crucial principle of 'Do no harm', described by Lichtman (2010: 54) as the 'cornerstone of ethical conduct'. There needs to be an expectation by those agreeing to participate in a research study that they will not be involved in any situation harmful to them. To ensure this happens five words are key:

- Confidentiality
- Anonymity
- Privacy
- Sensitivity
- Honesty.

We need to examine each of these briefly in turn.

- *Confidentiality*: There must be a clear understanding between both researchers and respondents, and a guarantee on behalf of you the researcher that all information collected about respondents will be given in confidence and only be used in terms agreed between both parties. This pledge is given at the start of research, when informed consent is being sought. A Case Example of a letter setting this out is given later in this chapter. The pledge of confidentiality extends to the undertaking that the data collected during the research will not be used for any other purpose than the one that was made clear when consent was given.
- *Anonymity*: All those consenting to participate in your research have the absolute right for their individual identities to remain known only to you, and the way this is done is through preserving their anonymity. Obviously, this is done by never revealing actual identities in the data collection or report writing. Most researchers do this by using 'Person A', 'Person B', etc., or giving fictitious names or referring only to employment roles.
- *Privacy*: The above two principles should guarantee the privacy of respondents but it is also important to respect that privacy beyond the research process. This means having no informal discussion about 'someone I interviewed' or even passing a likely contact to another researcher, without the respondent's permission.

- *Sensitivity*: You need to be sensitive to respondents' own situations and personal lives. The research should not be too intrusive; for example, not demanding too much of the respondents' personal time. Also, although a good rapport is essential between, say, interviewer and interviewee, you need to avoid a situation in which the interviewees believe they are actual friends of the researcher. An objective 'distance' must be maintained.

- *Honesty*: To avoid any possible misrepresentation about the accuracy of data collected personally from respondents, especially from interviewers, it is important that you the researcher and the respondent agree about what was actually said. You may well disagree over analysis and interpretation but you must not put yourself in a situation where the interviewee says 'I never said that!' Therefore, a copy of your record or transcript of the interview should be sent to the interviewee as soon as possible, giving them the chance to comment on its accuracy and perhaps suggest amendments. If the interviewee wants a slightly different version to the one you have sent, a compromise can normally be reached. If your two versions are a long way apart you may have to: (a) eliminate the interview from your research; (b) 'stick to your guns' – especially if you have an electronic recording; or (c) reach a compromise. We repeat that a complete disagreement is highly unlikely. The problem with all this is of course the time it takes to get approval from all interviewees, some of whom may be quite content with the record but forget to get back to you. It has become accepted practice that you are able to offer the interviewee a specific time within which to reply (say, five days maximum) and if no reply is received by that date, it can be taken that the record has been accepted as accurate. The note accompanying the record might read thus:

  I am confident you will find the summary an accurate record of the interview. However, if you do wish to comment or suggest some minor amendments, please get back to me within five days, i.e. by [date]. If I do not hear from you by then, I shall be happy to assume that you find the account accurate and you need take no action.

However, because the whole process involves fallible human beings (including you!), the above principles can still bring challenges to test your own ethical stance in carrying out your research. Here is a clear example:

During the course of the interview, the interviewer says 'I am going to tell you something off the record now ...' and goes on to tell you how he cheated in an examination or she falsified an application for the job she is doing now.

You have guaranteed confidentiality – do you maintain this or reveal the information to the appropriate authority? What about a student who reveals something that gives you concern about them? Again, the dilemma is the same.

The best advice is to head off such situations when you see them coming. 'Can we please keep to the agreed topic?' 'I'd rather you did not tell me anything off the record during this interview'. These are the phrases you might find useful. Of course, these situations are extremely unlikely to occur but they do illustrate that ultimately, whilst following official ethical procedures correctly, your own ethical framework will sometimes need to be applied. Another difficulty, discussed in Chapter Six, is that in any relatively small community, people sometimes find it relatively easy to identify a person, or even a school or a business from the information given. The authors of this book both worked on a Masters programme in the Seychelles, Africa's smallest nation state. Even in the whole country, especially when the programme had run for a few years, we found that some students were confident they knew the identities of various people described anonymously in other students' research! What you have to be certain of is that you personally have followed the procedures described above and are in no way responsible for any such identification.

Case example 5.2

For the final project of her Masters in Business Studies, Kate planned to research the extent to which environmentally 'green' issues were impacting on those working for public authorities.

Having selected her case study Local Authority, she wanted to send a questionnaire to a random sample of employees to discover how far their work had to take account of 'green' policies. She was to triangulate this with interviews of key personnel and documentary analysis of 'Town Hall' literature. Here is the letter she sent to the Chief Executive.

Address

Date

Dear _____

No one knows better than yourself the importance of environmental issues today, and I am writing to you to seek your support for my research into the way these are impacting upon Local Authority work.

I am in my final year of my Masters Degree in Business Studies at [name of institution] and hope to carry out this research for my final major project. Your Local Authority has a good record of supporting staff development so I hope you will be sympathetic to my request to send a questionnaire to a random sample of staff employed at Council Headquarters.

(Continued)

(Continued)

This questionnaire (of which I enclose a copy) will, as you will see, take staff no more than 15–20 minutes to complete and is non-intrusive. All data collected will be treated totally confidentially and, as you see, the questionnaire is to be anonymously completed. No individual(s) will be identified and the data will only be used in a collated form. The data will only be used for the purpose of my individual research and I will undertake to send you – and all those who request it – the collated results when they are complete. The Local Authority itself will not be named, unless you yourself request this when you have seen a copy of the final report.

If you agree to my request, I will send further copies of this questionnaire, on which I welcome your comments of course, to those selected employees.

I look forward to hearing from you and enclose a stamped addressed envelope for that purpose.

With best wishes.

Yours sincerely

Using specific research literature

In Chapter Three, we described how the literature review is used to examine the literature relating to your chosen research topic so that it sets the background into which your own research fits. There is of course another area of literature of which you need to show some knowledge and understanding – that which relates to research methodology. There are many books written about how to carry out research, some of them very academic, some more practical. Obviously, we believe the book you are now reading is an important part of that literature! In addition, the Further Reading texts at the end of this book's chapters provide further examples, as do the ones we have referenced in particular chapters, all of which are to be found in full in the References at the back of this book. Here, we simply need to draw to your attention that when you write in your final report of your project or dissertation, you need to demonstrate that you have read texts relating to research methodologies. For example, in describing the approaches to survey through questionnaires, the types of interviews, or the broad approaches to qualitative or quantitative research design, you need to reference your comments accordingly. We believe this book, some of the Further Reading texts and some of the book's references are adequate for this purpose. Just as in the main literature review, remember that not all research 'experts' agree! We noted above some of the different interpretations of 'validity' or 'reliability' that appear in the literature, for example, and tried to clarify these in a practical, helpful way. However, you may encounter firmly held contrasting views on particular approaches or methods. Our advice is to remember that there is no perfect research but to be confident that the approach and methods you have chosen *are* the most appropriate ones for your particular research.

Structuring your methodology section

Different HE institutions will have their specific individual requirements, as we note several times in this book. However, all of them require that you describe and justify how and why you have carried out the research that you have. This needs to be in a separate section of the final piece of work. The length of this section will again vary according to the individual institution's requirements of course, but for a typical 20,000-word dissertation or project report something between 3,000 and 5,000 words may be required. Make sure you check with your tutor, look at previous students' final reports and check the institution's requirements to see if a specific length for methodology is mentioned. Whatever the length, the following is a typical structure which would meet virtually all the requirements:

(i) A general introduction to the nature of the research, then a specific emphasis on research in your specific area, for example education, business studies, social sciences
(ii) Explanation of the different types of research
(iii) Description and explanation as to why the particular form of research was chosen for your study
(iv) Description and justification of the research instruments used in your study, clarifying why each is appropriate to the topic. Possibly mention some others that were considered and why they were ruled out, that is, why they were not suitable. Describe the piloting that occurred
(v) Description and justification of sample(s) used
(vi) Practical details of the numbers, non-responses, methods of recording
(vii) Consideration of how issues of validity, reliability and triangulation were addressed
(viii) Clarification of the ethical issues involved and how the methodologies took these into account.

Using this structure as a guideline, not as a straitjacket, should ensure you cover all the considerations that assessors are seeking.

Summary of Chapter Five

This chapter has:

- Described how to pilot research instruments
- Explained how an appropriate sample is decided upon
- Discussed the meaning of validity and reliability in research and the importance of triangulation
- Described how to ensure that appropriate ethical procedures are followed throughout the whole research process
- Commented on the need to use specific research literature
- Given advice on how to set out the methodology section of your dissertation or project report.

Further reading

De Laine, M. (2000) *Fieldwork: Participation and Practice: Ethics and Dilemmas in Qualitative Research*. London: Sage.

Denzin, N. and Lincoln, Y. (2000) *Handbook of Qualitative Research*. Thousand Oaks, CA: Sage.

6

Practitioner Research

Introduction

At the present time research into some element of your own work or aspects of your own organisation is increasing in popularity as many students want to make their work relevant to their own circumstances. There is a growing pressure to ensure that research is seen to have practical applications which will lead to improvement. Practitioner research provides you with the opportunity to relate your Masters Level programme to issues that directly impact on your own practice. This is an attractive option for many students who relish the opportunity to make a difference to their own performance or to their organisation, in both the public and private sectors. There is a need to ensure that this type of research is rigorous and meets the standards expected at this level. There are particular ethical issues associated with researching into your own practice or your own organisation. A particular method that is strongly associated with practitioner research is action research and we will spend some time in this chapter considering this method and other forms of practitioner research.

In this chapter the following topics are considered:

- The context of practitioner research
- Gaining access
- Carrying out reconnaissance
- Intervention
- Negotiation
- Monitoring
- Validation
- Ethical considerations.

Context of practitioner research

Action research is a method you will have encountered in your research methods course and, depending on your tutor and your higher education institution, it might be the dominant method. However, action research is only one aspect of the much broader area of practitioner research. We are concerned in this chapter with all aspects of research related to your own practice in your own organisation. This is a fairly broad definition, but the issues we raise will be useful when you consider your own research focus and will apply to a number of different situations across a range of organisations. There is a large amount of literature devoted to action research (see e.g., Altrichter et al., 2008; Koshy, 2009; McNiff and Whitehead, 2005, 2009a, 2009b; Reason and Bradbury, 2007; Somekh, 2006). Rather less emphasis is paid to the broader aspects of practitioner research (see e.g., Menter et al., 2010; Middlewood et al., 1999), but it is an important method you will want to consider when you start to think about your research approach. Practitioner research has a number of potential advantages:

- The research is based on real-life issues in your organisation.
- Your chosen area of investigation is interesting and relevant to you.
- It can lead to improvement in your own performance or within your organisation.
- Gathering data should be relatively straightforward.
- You have a good understanding of the research context.

To counter-balance these advantages there are also a number of disadvantages:

- It could be difficult to maintain objectivity during the project.
- There a number of ethical factors to be considered.
- You chose the topic because of pressure from your employing organisation.
- There is a potential conflict of interest.
- You may generate some difficult findings about your own practice or your organisation.

Gaining access

When you decide upon your topic for your research project one of the key factors is often the ease of access to data. Carrying out practitioner research should make access easier because you are investigating elements of your own practice or those of your organisation. Let us take two examples to illustrate the issues surrounding access.

Case example 6.1

Melanie, head of a history department in a large comprehensive school in the UK, decides to investigate how her own subject leadership can be improved. In particular she decides to investigate the following:

- The effectiveness of the departmental meetings she chairs every month
- The take-up by other members of staff of the new approaches to teaching and learning that have been introduced following discussion at the departmental meeting.

Case example 6.2

Vijay is a finance manager in a retail fashion company with six shops. He has identified two major issues concerning the training he provides to store managers regarding stock control procedures and the effectiveness of stock control in the shops. In particular he decides to investigate two particular aspects:

- The training programme he runs for store managers on stock control methods
- The supporting materials he provides to store managers to enable them to complete the stock control records.

In both cases there should be easy access to the data because the researcher is directly involved in the process. Background material should be readily available and specific information about the organisation should be easy to obtain. However, in both cases the researcher will be asking for feedback on their role from members of staff. Some members of staff may be reluctant to provide this data and even if they do they might not be open and honest. Of course, you can take steps to anonymise the data, but given the small scale of each organisation this might prove difficult in practice. Having an open and trusting relationship with colleagues will also help to reconcile these problems. However, consider how you would feel about giving honest feedback to your line manager. So, in practice, access might not be as straightforward as you first imagine. Reassuring colleagues that your work is for research purposes as part of your Masters programme and is not part of any 'check-ing up' on their work is crucial to gaining access. You have to ensure clear, consistent and honest communication is built into your overall approach. In the long-run secrecy will only create problems for you. Above all, remember that you cannot assume because you work in an organisation that access will not be an issue. You must always follow the correct procedures to ensure adequate access, and openness is always the best policy.

In the two Case Examples identified above, there are potential issues which might impede access. In both cases, the individual member of staff might consider they are being asked to comment on the performance of their line manager, or that their line manager is checking up on them. These factors might make access problematic. However, there are simple strat-egies to reconcile the concerns identified in the two Case Examples. The simplest way to deal with the issue of individual feedback is to take out the personal from the focus of the investigation. In the first Case Example the focus could shift more broadly onto the effective management of meet-ings and the development of new approaches to teaching and learning. In the second Case Example the focus moves onto developing more effective training and stock control methods, rather than the performance of Vijay the finance manager.

Reconnaissance

What we have outlined in the previous section is often described as part of the reconnaissance phase. This is the process of finding out about your piece of practitioner research. In particular your reconnaissance should enable you to:

- Find out more about the context of the research
- Find out about the focus of the research
- Identify what needs to change and therefore how to evaluate the change
- Develop a plan for action.

You will need to undertake this process a number of times to refine your research until you arrive at a suitable focus for your study. Once you have decided on the focus of your study the process of reconnaissance will not stop because other issues may arise that influence your proposed area of research. For example, in Case Example 6.2, the issues around stock control might be a symptom of deeper issues that are impacting on management in the business:

- What is the quality of the initial training given to managers?
- Is there a conflict between the fashion aspect of the shops and the business objectives?
- Do managers see any value in training?
- Do managers see any value in stock control?
- What stock control methods are managers actually using?
- Are there aspects of the entire stock control process that are more effective than others?

Whilst it might seem that this element of reconnaissance is actually making the process more complicated, it should, if done properly, enable you to identify the fundamental nature of the issue you want to investigate. So, in this case a more basic study of management selection and training within the organisation might be more appropriate. Getting the focus right at the outset will save time and reduce problems as you progress through your study. A grid, such as shown in Figure 6.1, might help you to simplify your reconnaissance phase.

Area of reconnaissance	What do I need to know?	Where will this come from?	How will I find out?
Initial training	Who does it and what is done?	Existing training programme	Documents and observation

Figure 6.1 Grid for reconnaissance phase of research

Once you have undertaken this initial phase of reconnaissance you will then be able to develop a series of ideas or hypotheses about the problem. This will enable you to begin to undertake some analysis of the issues involved. In Case Example 6.2 this could involve starting to consider the factors that influence management in the shops, such as the initial recruitment process, the level of training, or the nature of the stock control process.

Intervention

Having carried out a period of reconnaissance the next step is to decide upon the form your research will take. You may decide to undertake an evaluation of existing practice within your organisation, or you may decide to initiate some actions designed to improve practice. To return to the examples given earlier in the chapter, both of those are examples of an evaluation of existing practice. Melanie and Vijay are both attempting to investigate the existing situation in their organisation by gathering information on current practice. They would do this by employing some of the research methods described in Chapter Four. Following the collection and analysis of data it is likely that Melanie and Vijay will be in a position to put forward practical recommendations to improve performance within their organisation. Their intervention would consist of gathering data and involving individuals in the process who would be aware of the focus of the research. This may alert the organisation and the individuals to the issue, but any direct intervention to improve practice would only take place after the research has been completed.

An alternative to this approach is to build in some form of intervention into your own practice or some element of your organisation. This approach is commonly associated with the action research model and will require you to develop strategies to improve the issue you have identified. Let us return to the examples of Melanie and Vijay and reframe each focus to reflect this process and to introduce an initial action phase:

Case example 6.1

Melanie, head of a history department in a large comprehensive school in the UK, decides to investigate how her own subject leadership can be improved. In particular she decides to investigate the following:

- The effectiveness of the departmental meeting she chairs every month
- The take-up of other members of staff of the new approaches to teaching and learning that have been introduced.

As an initial action Melanie could decide to alter the format and structure of the departmental meeting by allowing other members of the department to chair the meeting and she could allow control of the agenda to pass from her to all the members of the department. This should make the whole process more democratic and give greater ownership of the meeting to the other members of the department. She can then find out if the new approach has been successful and it might also provide her with an improved understanding of the problem. For example she might find out that the real issue is not the meeting itself, but is related to more fundamental concerns about her leadership style. Melanie will then be in a position to further refine her research focus and move onto another cycle of research.

Case example 6.2

Vijay is a finance manager in a retail fashion company with six shops. He has identified a major issue concerning the training he provides to store managers to enable them to complete the stock control records. In particular he decides to investigate two particular aspects:

- The training programme he runs for store managers on stock control methods
- The supporting materials he provides to store managers to enable them to complete the stock control records.

There are a number of actions that Vijay could take to improve stock control across the group of six shops. An obvious change he could make would be to develop a new training programme for all shop managers on stock control. Vijay could instigate and run the revised training programme for the managers to see if a different approach to training improves the situation. Again, Vijay will be able to monitor the impact of this new programme and to see if it has had any effect on manager's attitudes and the physical process of stock control. The introduction of the new training programme might show, for example, that the problem lies not with the training itself, but with the negative attitude of the managers to any process instigated by head office associated with business management. Through this process Vijay will gain a greater understanding of the issue, the people he is working with and be able to further refine his research focus.

The approach we have outlined in both cases would be the first stage of an on-going process. This is usually referred to as a 'spiral of cycles' and involves a series of actions to improve a particular issue.

Negotiation

The process we have described in the previous sections will require negotiation with groups and individuals. This applies equally to the more narrow action research approach and the broader practitioner approach we have discussed. You may need to negotiate with other members of staff, or, if you work in an educational organisation, the students or parents. If possible you should concentrate on an area that you have ownership of, but in practice a number of stakeholders are likely to be involved in the process. You will be in the best position to judge what is acceptable within your organisation, but it is important to establish a clear protocol for negotiation with the various stakeholders. Negotiation will be an on-going process as your project develops and you will want to keep any stakeholders informed of the progress you are making.

If you are undertaking more general practitioner research you will need to negotiate access with the various stakeholders. This might involve seeking permission from your line manager to commence the project and getting the involvement of respondents for your data collection. Having a clear plan and programme will greatly improve the likelihood of people agreeing to provide you with the data you require. You have to get people to participate in your project and you will occasionally have to make compromises to ensure their participation. Dialogue is a key aspect of any successful practitioner research project. A summary document, of no more than one side of paper, explaining what you are doing, how you intend to do it and the purpose of the project will greatly facilitate the process. This summary is not meant to replace any negotiation you might undertake with individuals, rather it is to act as an aide-memoire for you. Remember, other people may not share your passion for the project and you need, where appropriate, to be concise and not waste their time with unnecessary explanations. Having a short outline to draw on will save time and ensure consistency.

If you are adopting an action research model you will also have to negotiate with any stakeholders who are going to be affected by the intervention you are planning. Even if you intend to make an alteration to some aspect of your own personal work you cannot assume this will not affect others. For example, if you are a teacher and you make changes to your classroom management strategies this might have an adverse impact on student outcomes and could lead to your head of department having to explain to the headteacher why results have dipped in the department. If the head of department has not been consulted about the changes made this could lead to problems for all parties.

Generally the bigger the change the wider the span of negotiation, so if as a teacher you decide to switch to another examination board for your General Certificate of Education (GCSE) class in an attempt to deal with underachievement you will need to negotiate at a number of levels across the school, and possibly with students and parents. The same principles will apply in business where a decision made by an individual may have far reaching consequences for other members of staff and the organisation as a whole. You need to consider the negotiations you will need to undertake before you begin the action research process, and of course you need to secure agreement from individuals before you can proceed with your plan of action. To do this effectively you will need to develop a plan of negotiation which will enable you to get to the right people at the right time. This plan will have to be

Proposed intervention	Stakeholders	Negotiation	Agreed action
Change examination board group	Headteacher	Discussion	Pilot one group
	Teachers	Discussion	
	Pupils	Information	
	Parents	Information	

Figure 6.2   Grid showing involvement of stakeholders

fluid because as the intervention develops more stakeholders might become involved and you may need to renegotiate the terms of your intervention. A grid (see Figure 6.2) will be useful.

Less negotiation will be required the smaller the intervention proposed and the more personal it is to your own practice. This should not be your prime consideration when deciding on your intervention, but it is something you will want to consider when you develop your project. However, do not assume that an intervention limited to your own personal practice will remove the need for negotiation. It is likely that someone else will be involved and the last thing you want is for someone else to be blamed for your actions.

Ethics are an important aspect of the negotiation process and we have looked at general ethical issues in Chapter Five. However, there are particular ethical concerns associated with practitioner research. You need to convince and reassure individuals involved in the research project that the information you are gathering is solely for research purposes and will not be used as a means of managing individual performance. You also then have certain responsibilities to deal with the data you have collected in a particular way.

Monitoring

As you embark on your practitioner research project you will have to establish a system that enables you to monitor the progress of your research and which tells you how well you are doing it. This is part of the broader process we mentioned earlier in the chapter related to refining your research as you move through the project. Monitoring is not just concerned with recording the progress of your project, and it has to have a positive and clearly defined purpose. In particular, it should be used to develop future action and to influence the focus and direction of your research project. Monitoring will involve utilising some of the research methods we have discussed in Chapter Four but your monitoring system will need to address a specific range of issues:

Activity	Time	Action	Outcome	Comments	Revision
Develop time plan	31 Sept.	Submit to tutor	Approved		None
Observe interviews	15 Oct.	Develop observation schedule	Observation	Problems with access to interviews	Inform HR
Evaluate observation	31 Oct.	Submit report to tutor	Arrange meeting with tutor		
Repeat observation	15 Nov.	Observe interviews	Observation	Inform HR	

Figure 6.3   Example of time plan

- The overall progress you are making
- The effect of your action
- Any additional or unexpected outcomes from your action
- What problems have you encountered?
- What solutions are you developing?

Part of this process may involve the construction of a working time plan. You might think this is an obvious part of the research process, but it is amazing how many students do not put this basic step in place. Of course there are fundamental time-related issues to consider when you develop a working time plan; for example, if your research involves school pupils you have to work with them before they leave, or if you are looking at a particular fixed-term initiative you will need to contact staff before their contract ends. You also need to ensure that you have sufficient time to carry out your research project and to meet the deadline imposed by your higher education institution. Many students set unrealistic targets, do not devote sufficient time to particular activities and find that they have run out of time. An effective working time plan for a study into staff recruitment, as shown in Figure 6.3, can help to overcome these problems.

An effective working time plan will enable you to discover potential blockages and also suggest solutions that will enable you to make progress. At the start of your research, when you were discussing your project with your tutor, you will probably have discussed a time plan working backwards from your estimated submission date. This will provide the starting point for your working time plan. However, what we are describing here is an organic plan that will grow and develop as your research progresses. Your working time plan has to be realistic, and it will have to be amended to reflect the actual progress you are making. The working time plan will act as an aide-memoire and provide you with a series of action points that can be used to influence the direction of your research project.

Validation

As you move through the research process you will move beyond merely monitoring the situation to actually providing some validation or explanation of the success or otherwise of your actions. You will do this by using a range of the research methods described in detail in Chapters Four and Five, for example, observation, interviewing. Bringing together information from a range of techniques, triangulation, enables you to compare and contrast the information available. In turn, this process will enable you to develop a greater insight into the problem you are researching. Putting your ideas into action will provide you with the opportunity to see what works in practice. You are concerned with observing and recording what changes your action brings about in the area you are interested in.

This process does seem relatively straightforward, but in practice you will discover it is not as simple as it seems. With action research your fundamental aim is to improve practice in the area you are investigating. You will also be aiming to increase your understanding of the area you are looking at. In an ideal world any action you choose to take will lead to certain outcomes, which will lead to an improvement in the situation and you will then be able to move on to the next phase of your action research. However, this linear process does not always work out smoothly and you might not get the positive result you envisaged. One action might not be enough to bring about the desired consequences and you may need to try a series of actions. Even if there is a positive outcome from your action there may be unintended negative consequences which lead you to revise your plans. Within action research you are constantly required to review and evaluate your actions. Elliot (1984: 75) writes about this process as 'the implementation and evaluation of action strategies as a form of hypotheses testing'. This process is an integral part of the action research cycle and it could continue indefinitely, but you have to be pragmatic because you only have a set time period to work in. This is a practical constraint on your work, but one that you have to operate with, even if you have not managed to solve all the problems and answer all the questions you have set yourself. There will come a point during your project where you have to stop, even if you feel there are unanswered questions or you could do more to improve the situation. You will also have to weigh up whether any further actions will lead to any potential future benefits. This is perfectly acceptable in action research provided you explain the context and the stage which your research has reached.

Undertaking the validation process, by putting your ideas into action and recording and reflecting on the outcomes, will provide you with the necessary evidence to decide which changes to make to your project. Validation will give you the authority to move your project forward and eventually it will give you the justification to bring the project to an end.

Ethics

Chapter Five gave an overview of the ethical issues surrounding your project in leadership and management. However, there are a number of specific ethical elements related to practitioner research and to action research in particular (Campbell and Groundwater-Smith, 2007).

Any research project which involves conducting research in your workplace will require careful consideration. As we have pointed out earlier in the chapter, researching into your colleagues' professional activities might create certain tensions and will require sensitive approaches to a number of issues. The relatively small-scale nature of practitioner research can create particular problems because it is often difficult to disguise the identity of individual participants. It is sensible to lay down particular ethical guidelines when you commence the research project. You will normally be required to complete an ethical approval form before you commence your research. We have included an illustrative example of an ethical form – Figure 6.4.

The ethical form will provide the basis for the discussions you will have with research participants. To reassure the participants and to help you complete the ethical form the establishment of a series of guiding principles will be useful:

Confidentiality: You will collect a range of data and you will need to be sensitive to those who have provided the data and about how you use it. It is important to remember that the ownership of the data lies with those who have provided it. To ensure the openness and commitment of participants at all times you will need to maintain confidentiality and reassure the respondents that you will continue to maintain this confidentiality. If you fail to convince participants of the confidential nature of your research you will find it difficult to gather appropriate data. You will also need to make clear to participants that you will not discuss who has provided the data with anyone else, and you would not provide data to a third party without prior agreement of the person who has provided the data. If you are employed in the organisation you are carrying out the research in, you may come under pressure from managers to reveal the names of those who have provided the data, but you must resist this pressure.

APPLICATION FOR ETHICAL APPROVAL FORM

NEED TO FILL OUT DETAILS

Name of student:

Student ID number:

Course:

Dissertation/project title:

Supervisor:

Participants (if children, specify age range) AND ATTACH A COPY OF YOUR CRB CLEARANCE:

Consent – will prior informed consent be obtained?

From participants?   YES/NO

From others?   YES/NO

Explain how this will be obtained. If prior informed consent is not to be obtained, explain why:

Will participants be explicitly informed of your status?   YES/NO

Confidentiality

Will confidentiality be maintained?   YES/NO

How will confidentiality be ensured?

Protection of participants

How is the safety and well-being of participants to be ensured?

Is information gathered from participants of a sensitive or personal nature?   YES/NO

(Continued)

If yes, describe the procedure for:

(a) ensuring confidentiality

(b) protecting participants from embarrassment or stress

Observational research

If observational research is to be carried out without prior consent of participants, please specify:

(a) situations to be observed

(b) how will privacy and cultural and religious values of participants be taken into account?

Signed (Student):   Date:

Signed (Supervisor):   Date:

Action: Once both you and your supervisor have signed this form take it to your course administrator. If there are any queries, these will be logged and the form sent back to you for amendment and re-submission. Otherwise the form will be signed by your course leader and you will be able to collect a signed copy from your course administrator. The signed copy should be included as an appendix in your assignment/thesis.

COURSE LEADER TO COMPLETE

☐   Approved

☐   Approved with modification or conditions – see below

☐   Action deferred. Please supply additional information or clarification – see below

Course Leader Name:

Signed: Date:

Figure 6.4   Example of ethical approval form

Anonymity: You will need to use the data you have collected when you come to write up your project and normally you would not identify people who have taken part in the research. An important aspect of retaining the confidence of those who have provided the data is to ensure that their true identities are disguised. This will improve the likelihood that they will be open and honest in their responses to the questions you may ask. The use of pseudonyms will enable you to do this, but it is sometimes difficult to retain anonymity when there is only a small sample from one particular organisation. It is important that you remain sensitive to this issue, even if you have changed names and disguised locations.

Negotiation: You will need to continue to negotiate with the people who have participated in the research. Initially you will have to negotiate access to enable you to carry out your project and the guidelines we have been describing here will be useful in the initial phase to lay down clear parameters of the process. You will need to think about which individuals and groups you need to negotiate with and this will be an on-going process as your research develops. Do not just focus on the immediate participant, and make sure you think carefully about the wider impact of your research. You will have to decide how far you go with the process of negotiation, but the process should be repeated at each stage of your research and with different groups and individuals. You will need to allow individuals time to think about their response to your request to use specific data. You have to accept that, in rare cases, some people may be reluctant to agree to your research approach or may refuse your request to use the data they have provided. Remember if you are refused access or required to adapt your methodology you have to agree to the participants' demands because they own the data. It is in your interests to secure agreement, so you have to accept their views. If you fail to get agreement you will have to change the focus of your research. However, it is very unusual to encounter problems or to fail to secure agreement if you have explained the research process and purpose to participants clearly and properly at the outset. In most cases participants will be keen to take part in your project, especially if the research will have a positive impact on their practice.

Feedback: Ensure that you agree with participants what feedback you will provide to them regarding the research. Establish clear protocols for checking data and gaining permission to use data. Whilst this is part of the negotiation process, and you will explain this at the outset, it is easy to forget this once you've collected the data. Once you have completed one part of the research your focus naturally tends to move to the next stage and it is easy to forget the protocols you have agreed. However, if people have agreed to co-operate with you as part of the data collection exercise you have a responsibility to maintain your part of the bargain and provide proper feedback to them. This is an important part of the ethical process and is one that can often be overlooked because of the time pressures facing the researcher. Research participants will be interested to check what you have collected, as well as how you intend to use it in your final writing up, so do not forget the importance of regular feedback. You should take control of the feedback and participants should not have to contact you to find out what has happened to their interview.

Control: If you are adopting an action research approach it is important that you recognise the importance of the other individuals who are taking part in the research. We said earlier in the chapter that action research involves some form of intervention in your own practice or some element of your organisation. If, for example, you are looking at improving elements of your leadership within your area of work you will need to fully involve those you work with. In effect, they will have some control over the situation because they are part of the process. Allowing participants to have some degree of control is often difficult because as the researcher you have a natural desire to retain control. You may view the research as your property, but within action research, control has to be shared with the participants who will be affected by the outcome of the work.

Establishing an effective set of ethical guidelines at the start of your research will help to prevent the development of problems in the future. Openness is really the best policy to ensure proper and continuing access. You have to be responsive to the needs of the other people involved in the research and you have to maintain a dialogue to ensure agreement. Circumstances can change and you have to be aware of the need to continue to talk and listen to the people you are working with.

The 'golden rule' here is:

Ethical considerations are an important part of your research and remember never to take access to or the co-operation of participants for granted. Continue to keep people informed of your progress and at all times maintain an open dialogue with all participants.

 Summary of Chapter Six

This chapter has:

- Identified the overall purpose and structure of practitioner research
- Explored the main issues associated with action research
- Discussed the elements necessary to develop a practitioner research approach
- Provided an introduction to the development of a series of ethical principles to underpin your research project.

Further reading

Coghlan, D. and Brannick, T. (2009) *Doing Action Research in Your Own Organization*. London: Sage.

Middlewood, D., Coleman, M. and Lumby, J. (1999) *Practitioner Research in Education*. London: Paul Chapman Publishing.

7

Presenting and Analysing Data

When the research methods have been applied, you will have your data collected. Now comes one of the most crucial parts of the process, where you in effect ask the question, 'What do I make of what I have found?' Your analysis and interpretation of what you have found will be an area that will be studied very closely. This in itself is made easier – for you and others – by the way in which the data is actually presented. This chapter therefore considers the following:

- The overall structure of this section
- How quantitative data may be presented
- How qualitative data may be presented
- Guidance on the analysis of quantitative data
- Guidance on the analysis of qualitative data
- Analysis of all the data
- The importance of self-criticism of findings
- Writing your conclusions, following analysis and interpretation
- Making recommendations.

The structure of this section

There is one overriding principle to remember in presenting and analysing data – our next 'golden rule':

Ensure you keep the presentation of your data separate from your analysis.

The reason for this is not only that it actually makes your own analysis easier to do when all the data is presented together, but, more importantly, different people can reach different conclusions when they analyse the same data. In order to give the assessors, and any other readers, the opportunity to reach their own conclusions based upon their own analyses, you need to show the data clearly in a form that is the same to everyone. In other words, we can all look at the same evidence but we may analyse that evidence differently, rather as in the case of legal proceedings. If you confuse the issue by offering some data with analysis attached, it is much more difficult to be objective about the data's whole picture.

The structure of this part of your project is therefore likely to be as follows, after the section on methodology.

Presentation and analysis of data section

1. Data presentation

   - Data from questionnaires to students
   - Data from interviews with leaders
   - Data from respondents' time logs.

   (These are examples of course; the point is to present data collected via each research instrument separately.)

2. Data analysis

   - Analysis of questionnaire responses
   - Analysis of interviews
   - Analysis of observation findings.

   (Again, these are examples. Note that if you have used the same instrument with different respondents, list these separately but consecutively, e.g.:

   - Data from questionnaires to middle managers
   - Data from questionnaires to senior managers.)

Conclusions and recommendations section

Occasionally, these two headings will be required as separate sections, so check your own institution's regulations to see if this is the case.

As you know from your experience and from earlier chapters in this book, data will basically be of either a quantitative or a qualitative nature, and most likely you will have a mixture of both kinds. As they require different kinds of both presentation and analysis, it is sensible to discuss each separately.

Presentation of quantitative data

Since there are specialist textbooks on the area of quantitative data presentation and analysis (see Further Reading), we restrict ourselves here to focusing on what most Masters Level students will find helpful. Those with a specific mathematical or statistical ability and enthusiasm will wish to go much further. For many students, there are also computer software packages which will be useful in these analyses.

Basically, a high standard of presentation of quantitative data is achieved by most Masters Level students simply through the use of what is known as descriptive statistics. This involves using graphics with which everyone is familiar, such as:

- Bar charts
- Pie charts
- Frequency tables
- Histograms
- Various tables involving lists of returns.

Some graphics are more suitable than others for particular kinds of data. For example, a pie chart is often suitable for nominal data (where a simple category is listed) but not for ordinal data (where an order or ranking has been required).

If we take a simple, and very common, example of the presentation of the data from questionnaires sent to a sample of respondents, we can see that the effective presentation of the data received may depend on the nature of the questions asked. Remember that we made the point in Chapter Four that in devising your questionnaire you should think carefully *at that stage* about the form in which the data from the replies might lend itself to analysis. If one question in your instrument asked respondents to tick a box indicating whether the most effective training they received was primarily from:

Senior managers ☐ Peer colleagues ☐ Immediate superior ☐
External agency ☐

The numbers could be received and presented as in Table 7.1.

Table 7.1 Example of nominal data presentation

Source of training	Numbers
Immediate superior	31
External agency	24
Peer colleagues	19
Senior managers	11
Total	85

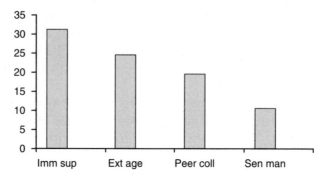

Figure 7.1   Nominal data as a bar chart

However, the data could probably be shown in a visually more compelling way as a bar chart – Figure 7.1.

If the same question had been asked of two or more different groups, the bar chart could be modified so that different numbers for each group could be shown by adjacent blocks, perhaps using different colours (even black and white at the simplest level!). You still need to ensure that you have given the actual total (in our example, 85) of replies received which are used in the presentation graphic.

It is important to ensure the reader of your project is given the information about numbers of those who did not return the questionnaire or only partly completed it. Gray (2009: 456–7) gives a very helpful way of classifying this missing data as:

'Not applicable' (NA) – for example, when the wrong person has replied.
'Refused' (R) – when a blunt refusal or rude answer is given.
'Did not know' (DK) – when a question is deliberately left blank while others had been accurately completed.
'Forgot to answer' (FA) – when all questions are answered except one.

As he points out, 'if many people fail to answer the same question, this might suggest there is something about the question they do not like – in which case, this could be construed as refusal' (Gray, 2009: 457).

Again, we are reminded of the importance of piloting, as described in Chapter Five. This piloting should have eliminated the reason for people not answering because it was an obscure or badly worded question. It becomes safe therefore to deduce that the reason for not answering was a definite refusal (such as it reflected upon themselves in a negative way).

You may therefore end with a series of graphic illustrations, depicting your quantitative data. Each separate graphic must be carefully numbered and labelled, even if you have stated, for example, that 'The replies from the sales representatives are shown in Figure 4.1'.

Note that each figure is numbered according to the chapter or section of the project first, then the order within the chapter or section. Thus if Chapter Four of your project is 'Data Presentation and Analysis', the figures will be labelled 4.1, 4.2, 4.3, and so on. You should still put a label or heading on the figure, such as in our example: 'Figure 4.1 Replies from questionnaire to sales representatives'.

After each figure or sometimes set of figures, it can be appropriate to insert brief comments on the data presented to highlight points that you wish to draw to the reader's attention. It is very important that these are exactly that – comments, and not analysis, which comes later! In the example concerning effective training given earlier, it is possible to comment that:

> Those believing the most effective training came from their immediate superiors were nearly three times as many as those believing it came from senior managers.

It is *not* appropriate to say, for example:

> It is very surprising that so few people nominated senior managers as delivering effective training – only a third of those who preferred their immediate superiors.

The phrase 'very surprising' is subjective – you are making a judgement and therefore such comments belong in the analysis, where you will be putting forward your reasons as to why it is surprising.

An important aspect of analysis, as we shall see, can be comparison. If the data justify it, it is possible to point in your comments to the contrast between two sets of returns as shown in your graphics. Again, you are simply noting that the figures contrast but not analysing how or why.

To sum up, presentations of your quantitative data are almost certain to involve the use of tables, charts and other graphics to display the figures in an accessible way – lending them available to either detailed inferential statistical analysis or more straightforward analysis, depending on our own interest and ability and the nature of the data.

Presentation of qualitative data

The qualitative data you collect is likely to come from such sources as interviews you have carried out, documents you have read for analysis, or copies of diaries, journals and logs that you have commissioned. In these and similar processes the data does not take the form of a number, a tick in a box, completing a form, etc., but involves pieces of writing, usually continuous prose, and some of it lengthy. In all these cases, you will have studied a number of documents which may add up to several thousand words, for example:

- Transcripts of all the interviews carried out (either from notes or recordings)
- Actual diaries or field notes, from various people
- Documents in their original form which you have selected
- Notes you have taken during observations.

Apart from the documents in their original form, these records will each have had some kind of structure imposed which you, the researcher, devised, such as the questions forming the interview schedule, the framework of the diary used, the headings used in the time log, the schedule for the observation. Again, when you devised these, you were already thinking of the form in which the data would arrive (see Chapter Four again). It is these structures which you need to bear in mind as you present the data from the instrument concerned. Let us consider the presentation of data from semi-structured interviews.

Firstly, in recording and storing the data you should have:

- put all materials in a similar format
- recorded your own initial comments/reflections alongside
- coded each separate piece for identification
- made a back-up copy of all original material

(Denscombe, 1998: 209–10).

Next, avoid at all costs the presenting of interviewee responses in a 'list' format. This is extremely tedious to read. An assessor's heart will sink when (s)he reads the following about the data from six interviews about the management of the implementation of a national policy at institutional level.

Question One: Four of the six said that they agreed that the policy was fair. One said she felt it was only fair to some staff. The remaining interviewee said that the policy was unfair to the majority of people.

Question Two: All the interviewees said that the implementation of the policy had gone smoothly, with few problems.

Question Three: Three thought the support from the Ministry had been adequate, whilst three others thought it had been unhelpful.

And so on. Of course, the answers are normally longer than these, but the repetition in the presentation format leads to boredom and is unhelpful in preparing for the analysis section.

As it was yourself who devised the interview schedule, you will have had in mind particular themes which you wanted to explore in finding out interviewees' answers to questions about the topic. What you are able to do here, in presenting the interview data is to use those themes as the sub-headings for your data. Thus, your themes for the above example on a policy might have included: fairness, implementation, support from policy makers, key elements in policy effectiveness, barriers to success, overall impact and prospects for the future. For example:

Data from interviews with institutional leaders. Six semi-structured interviews were carried out using the schedule described in Section 3 (a copy of the schedule is in Appendix 2). These are the findings from the interviews.

(a) Fairness of the policy

Four of the interviewees had no significant complaints about the policy's fairness. Although there were details to be improved upon these four all felt that the policy affected most people equally, some to people's slight detriment, some to their favour. The leader of Institution B however felt that the policy emerged significantly in favour of those staff who remained with a company for 10 years or more and those in their early years with a company were disadvantaged. This leader felt that the policy would eventually discriminate against 'go ahead', relatively mobile workers. The leader of C was the most critical, believing that the policy discriminated against the majority of staff in C and that there would be a detrimental impact on recruitment, unless adjustments were made.

(b) Implementation of the policy

[In a similar way.]

(c) Key elements in policy effectiveness

[And so on ...]

This format, using your own themes, gives you ample scope when you come to the detailed analysis. Notice that the reference to specific institutions above prepares the way for you to analyse the policy according to the different impact it makes on different institutions. The leaders are seeing the policy from that specific perspective; you will have the opportunity, having analysed all six sets of interview data, to reflect on how important this is – whether it is the policy itself or the way it is dealt with in specific institutions.

Presenting data from other sources

In the case of observations, you will have described the sample of meetings chosen, the reasons why they were chosen and the observation schedule construction in the Methodology section of your project. Thus your section on data can be straightforward, such as:

Data from observation of meetings

Four meetings were observed, using the observation schedule described earlier (a copy of this is in Appendix C).

Reason(s) for the meetings and agendas

Three of the four meetings were simply as regularly designated by the college's calendar, held on the first Tuesday of each month. The agendas in two of these three were designated by the College Leadership Team as a list of eight topics that needed to be considered by the departments. The other of these three had given items prescribed but were able to include other agenda items that had been deemed important by the departmental head. The fourth meeting had an agenda which was of the department's own devising, with three items being put forward by its head, and the remaining five proposed prior to the meeting by departmental members. The designated items were all relating to policy matters, either at national or regional level. The agenda items proposed by departmental heads all related to departmental policies and processes; the items proposed by members related to individual staff responsibilities, student behaviour and security issues.

Conduct and organisation of the meetings

[And so on ...]

As far as presenting data from diaries or time logs is concerned, the headings that you have designated for respondents to complete their entries under could be a very helpful way of presenting the data here.

With documents in their original form, over which you had no control, such as staff handbooks, job descriptions, recruitment booklets, and so on, your task is to impose a structure which gives you scope for analysis, such as particular sections in common, length of sections, overall format, and so on.

With qualitative data, you will have noted that you are including your comments in the data and do not have to add them separately as you do with quantitative tables, lists and the like.

Analysis of quantitative data

As noted earlier, detailed and more complex statistical analysis techniques can be studied elsewhere. A concise and very readable source is by Pell and Fogelman (2002: 235–61), which covers all the essential approaches in this area. Here, we confine ourselves to the analysis of descriptive statistics.

Of the two types of data referred to earlier, nominal and ordinal, nominal will almost certainly have been presented in graphics such as tables and charts. Ordinal data may well have involved use of a Likert scale, described in Chapter Four. Here, it can be helpful to work out the mean level of agreement with a particular statement using your figures of 'Strongly Agree', 'Agree', 'Disagree' and 'Strongly Disagree', it is a helpful way of understanding the data. To give a simple example:

Strongly Agree	58
Agree	25
Disagree	12
Strongly Disagree	5
Total	100

Strongly Disagree	$5 \times 1 =$	5
Disagree	$12 \times 2 =$	24
Agree	$25 \times 3 =$	75
Strongly Agree	$58 \times 4 =$	232
Total		336
Mean (336/100)	$= 3.36$	

Using this simple example, we can also see that 17% did not agree with the statement (either 'strongly' or not), and 83% did agree (either 'strongly' or not).

The data from prioritising questions referred to in Chapter Four, can also provide detailed yet simple statistics for analysis, as can asking respondents to give scores for certain aspects in your research questions. For those with basic mathematical skills, these enable you to consider and analyse things such as:

- The distribution – taking into account the normal 'bell-shaped' distribution, and considering deviation above or below the mean
- The range – between the lowest and highest scores.

Such basic statistics are quite acceptable for analysis of, for example, the results of a survey. Indeed, if the numbers involved are small, it is better to avoid anything at all complex. Forcing small figures into percentages, for example, is not sensible and looks as false as it actually is. If two out of six people claim something is true, we advise against saying that '33% agreed'!

All data are likely to be *classified* based on your own returns from your research instruments. It can also involve *comparison* where two or more sets of data being compared can offer interesting insights.

Often such data sets have been accumulated through the researcher's need to acquire respondent triangulation (see Chapter Four), ascertaining whether different perceptions of the same issue exist, depending upon the viewpoint of the particular respondent. Earlier (Case Example 2.1) we saw how different perceptions of how much and how often praise by managers was offered. If a similar topic was researched in a school, the respondents concerned would be classroom teachers and school children. Two sets of data might be gained in which the mean score of agreement with the statement 'Teachers praise pupils regularly for good work' was 3.4 for the teachers and 1.7 for the pupils. Whilst this is clearly a significant difference, you would know that there are many more pupils than teachers in a school, probably one teacher for every 30 or so pupils. Therefore, there would be a need to examine other factors in the situation of relationships between those teachers and those pupils before reaching conclusions.

Another example producing several data sets for respondent triangulation came from a piece of student research on team working. Two sets of respondents (managers and workers) were asked to prioritise nine factors in effective team working, numbering them 1 to 9. Analysis and comparison of the two initial data sets showed the responses were very similar, especially in identifying the three most important factors and the three least important ones. However, when the two sets of respondents were asked to assess which factors could be most readily seen in actual practice at work, the data showed a marked divergence, with a number of workers identifying some of the least important factors as being most prevalent, and the most important non-existent. The four sets of data therefore lent themselves to a good deal of comparison and cross referencing in analysis such as:

- Workers' theoretical factors compared with the actual practice
- Managers' theoretical factors compared with the actual practice
- Workers' theoretical factors compared with managers' theoretical factors
- Workers' actual practice compared with managers' actual practice
- Discrepancy/agreement between workers' own theoretical practice and their perception of actual practice compared with the same discrepancy/agreement for the managers.

To summarise, therefore, collecting statistics from survey instruments especially can provide data which offers an opportunity for analysis at a relatively straightforward mathematical level, using only descriptive statistics.

Analysis of qualitative data

Whereas quantitative data provides precise facts and figures, qualitative data, because it is concerned with opinions, perceptions and interpretations of people, is more concerned with understanding and meaning than with fact. As Watling (2002: 267) points out, the qualitative data analyser has to make choices, about what to leave out and what to include. This in itself is an act of analysis. A good example is in interviewing. When you ask someone a question, you can record the words spoken as an answer. How do you take account of such factors as:

- Tone of voice (e.g. when the interviewee becomes excited)?
- Posture (e.g. the way the interviewee sits – relaxed or tense)?
- Facial expression (e.g. scowling, smiling)?
- Gesticulating (e.g. pointing finger, slapping desk)?

Is it possible to take account of these? You need of course to have decided in creating your research instrument whether to include such things or not, and how to record them, but there remains a strong element of subjectivity in this.

In suggesting the need for avoidance of repetitive listing in qualitative data presentation, we recommended the noting of themes or topics as a way of marshalling the data. Each theme having been coded in your records, the analysis now becomes much more accessible, although you may refine or adjust your original thematic headings. In analysing qualitative data, there still remains a need to be systematic, in effect applying quantitative analysis. The best example of this is content analysis.

Content analysis involves counting and analysing the frequency of certain words or phrases. In prepared questions for an interview schedule, it is possible to code in advance certain key words. However, in an answer to an open question 'What are your views on _____?', this is not possible. Content analysis is widely used in documentary research, and of course transcripts of interviews are, of necessity, documents. It has been suggested that there are three crucial steps, namely: sampling, recording and categorising.

In analysing documents we can adopt Cortazzi's (2002) advice about narratives to ask key questions about the documents:

- What kind of documents are these?
- What is the purpose of the document?
- How can the documents be compared?
- Does the document provide its own context?
- What is the relationship between the writer and the reader(s)?
- How can my analysis represent the human qualities involved?
- Which criteria do I use to assess the document's worth?

In attempting to answer these questions, you will find you have a sound framework for producing an analysis of the data in the documents. This framework sometimes can be developed by deciding upon an order of importance of categories or headings that you decide upon. This *may* well correspond to the number of times a key word or phrase suggesting this category occurs, but this is not always so. In qualitative analysis, unlike quantitative, you can make a judgement about importance and, as long as this is based on data, this is what matters. After all, people can mean different things by different words. Consider, for example, the words 'appraisal', 'assess', 'evaluate', 'review', all of which broadly relate to the same areas of management. A mere counting of those individual words would not necessarily give you the order of importance of a category.

When you have concluded your draft of the analysis of a set of interview transcripts or documents and gained your interpretation as to the meaning they provided, then it is important to go back and test your meanings or interpretations against the data. If the data support is questionable, return to your analysis. Resist the temptation at this stage to force the meaning from the data or, even worse, force the data to fit the meaning. Some analysts, such as Lichtman (2009: 200), consider the final stage of qualitative analysis to be 'from categories to concepts' and suggest that a small number of well developed and supported concepts is to be preferred to a lengthy list of concepts. We tend to agree with this. Lichtman suggests five to seven concepts as a rule of thumb.

The phrase 'grounded theory' is one which you are likely to encounter in the field of qualitative data. Entire books have been written about grounded theory and you may read about it in those but, generally speaking, it is most usefully applied at Doctoral or professional research level. In simple terms, grounded theory is about collecting data with no preconceived ideas, then beginning to form ideas or theories from this open data, and then use those as the basis for continuing later data collection. For example, the researcher might begin with 'open discussions' with respondents about a broad area of their work or lives. From examination of data from these discussion, patterns might be found which could form the basis of future interviews with other respondents. Apart from an initial lack of structure, the amount of time taken can be considerable and is not usually suitable for someone trying to achieve a Masters Level project or dissertation in a year.

Analysis of ALL the data

When you have analysed all the separate sets of data, it will be useful to write a section in which you bring together an analysis of all the data before you turn to your conclusions. Let us suppose that you have collected data from several sources (respondent triangulation) and used more than one research instrument (methodological triangulation). For example you have data from:

(i) A questionnaire to respondents X
(ii) A questionnaire to respondents Y
(iii) Interviews with respondents Z
(iv) Analysis of certain relevant documents.

You will have presented an analysis of data from (i) and from (ii). You will have compared the two data sets. You will have analysed (iii) and then analysed (iv). You now need to ask the question 'What does all the data – from (i), (ii), (iii) and (iv) – tell us?'

First of all, look back and remind yourself of the original key purpose of your research project. What were you trying to discover? If some of these data from different sources seem contradictory, so be it! After checking your separate analyses carefully, look for patterns which have something in common across all the data and then examine areas which are less in agreement.

 Case example 7.1

Veatriki, a Greek student, studying for her Masters in Educational Leadership and writing in English as her second language, researched the effectiveness of the recruitment process in Greek and English schools using a multi-case-study approach. This is the final section of her dissertation chapter in which she presented and analysed her data.

Total data analysis

Whilst the data from the questionnaires to teachers in the Greek schools showed that their perceptions of the process were predominantly of a lack of fairness and on ignoring individuality, the perceptions of the managers involved, according to the data, suggested that they were mainly satisfied with the process. In the English schools, the data analysis of parallel questionnaires revealed that the perceptions of both teachers and managers were very similar. Despite misgivings about the variability of processes, both sets of respondents felt they were mostly fair and tried to allow for individuality.

(Continued)

(Continued)

The analysis of the recruitment documentation and linked job descriptions showed that whilst several stated aims of recruitment were similar, there were wide differences in expectations of teachers appointed. Analysis of the total data gives a picture of contrasting expectations, reflecting the different nature of the Greek and English education systems, with the former highly centralised and the latter very de-centralised. The data overall draws attention to the disparity between the views of the appointing bodies and the applicants in Greece, whereas in England there is much greater agreement between these. Whatever the merits or demerits of either system, therefore, this difference may be seen as significant for those examining the effectiveness of the recruitment process.

Write an accurate and truthful analysis of what the data shows. Before moving to drawing – and setting out – your conclusions, however, you should ensure that you follow this 'golden rule':

Be self critical and aware of the limitations of your research.

Being self-critical

In Chapter Five, we described the importance of ensuring the reliability and validity of your data. You have done this partly by ensuring the use of triangulation. Now is the time to apply a final checklist to what you have done. Check that:

- Each of your research instruments was meticulously applied, technically and ethically as well as consistently, to all those concerned.
- The sample used in each case was appropriate for your evidence to be seen as valid. For example, were there sufficient interviews or documents or observations and did they give a sufficient sample of the *range* of personnel/papers/events needed.
- Your findings are not likely to represent a quirk or 'freak'. For example, were your interviews/observations conducted at a time when things were 'normal' – in the sense of what is usual for the organisation or people. If not, your data may not be able to be seen as helpful.

This list covers what we may call any *technical* limitations that you should be ready to draw to the reader's attention. Credit is always given to research students who show they are aware that their research is not perfect and could have been improved in some way. This shows they are learning as researchers.

The second set of potential limitations to the validity of your research is more challenging, as these involve your personal attitudes and values. You should ask yourself:

- Have I ensured that my own personal values and context have not in any way distorted my findings and analysis? This is not likely to be intentional of course, but you could reflect on whether your professional context and career values have at all affected your thinking in the analysis.
- Am I confident that any awareness of what my sponsors would ideally like from my research findings has not influenced my analysis?

If you have doubts about either of these, go back and reflect and if necessary amend. In writing a brief section on potential limitations of the findings analysis, a statement such as the following (an actual one) is acceptable.

Whilst the sample of interviewees cannot be claimed to represent the full range of managers in the company, the researcher believes the data gives a sufficient picture of attitudes within the managerial level for conclusions to be drawn. The researcher has made every effort to ensure that his own position in the company (see Section A) has not influenced his ability to be objective.

Setting out the conclusions

Conclusions are not just a way of rounding off the findings of your research. The conclusions section gives you the opportunity to step back from all the analyses of all the findings and reflect on what may be concluded from the whole work. It should not therefore merely repeat the findings from the analysis, but try to put forward some statements about what can be reasonably deduced from the research evidence. It is important in setting out conclusions that you:

- Remind yourself for whom the research report is intended
- Relate back to the original research aims set out earlier in the purpose statement(s) near the beginning of the project
- Ensure that everything you state as a conclusion can be referred back to evidence, if required, in your findings.

It is surprising how many books on research actually omit mention of conclusions, relying on analysis and the ensuing findings as forming the end. In fact, academic assessors will need to know whether you can draw out reasonably succinct conclusions, and set them out.

In addition to academic assessors, others who may have a legitimate interest in the research (especially sponsors) will expect to see a firm set of conclusions – they may not be interested in all the detail *until* they have read the conclusions in fact! Your ability to reach the audience for whom the research is intended can be tested in your ability to write a succinct but attention-grasping conclusion section.

While there are those (e.g. James et al., 2008: 184) who advocate that the conclusion is where the 'passion' of the practitioner needs to show, we would propose a measured response – statements which will stand up to the close scrutiny of supporting evidence. However, they do need to be strong statements and where the evidence from the research findings analysis is equivocal, then it is important not to stretch credibility by making suppositions.

A conclusion might be as follows (from a Masters Level study by Phoebe into the effectiveness of induction programmes for graduate employees):

> The study showed clearly that a carefully managed and regularly updated induction programme for new graduate employees had a beneficial impact on retaining those staff for a sufficient period for them to make a useful contribution to the company's development. It was not possible to conclude that the same impact would be achievable for non-graduate employees.

The conclusions section, although relatively brief, is so important in terms of its potential impact that it is worthwhile:

- Writing a series of draft statements, then
- Checking each one against the original purpose statement(s), then
- Checking that there is precise evidence in the findings that can be elicited to support the conclusion statement, then
- Re-drafting the statements into a final form.

What about if you want to propose a theory or model, based upon what you have found? The key here is not to be too assertive or over-confident about your theory. Do not expect to identify a single definite reason why, for example, a particular leadership approach failed or succeeded. Did it, according to your data, make a 'noticeable' or 'significant' impact?

The other point to remember, as Popper (1968) pointed out, is that there are no guarantees in theories – only that the evidence may show that they may be right – for the time being. Something may occur in the future that shows the theory is no longer true.

With that in mind, by all means propose the theory that the data suggests to you.

Case example 7.2

In her research for her MBA, Brenda's purpose had been to investigate whether the integration of her Accountancy Department into a Business Studies Faculty in the Further Education College where she worked had resulted in higher quality teaching and learning in the subject. Following the analysis of a large amount of data, both quantitative and qualitative, her conclusions were:

'Conclusions

Although the amalgamation of the Accountancy Department was not welcomed by the Accountancy staff, as shown by the questionnaire data, there was an acceptance of the need for the change. Indeed, the data indicated that, despite their reservations on a personal level, the very skills inherent in the staff's work enabled them to see the logic of the amalgamation.

Analysis of the test and examination results showed that these remained stable, and accepted as "Good", after the change. Arguments can be made that maintaining this quality is a positive after an unsettling change, although some Faculty members felt the results should have significantly improved.

Feedback from student learners suggested that they remained positive about their results, but that the quality of the teaching remained variable as previously.

There is evidence that staff relationships within the new Faculty have begun to develop positively and that the increased training now on offer to Accountancy staff will lead to overall improvement. Less effective teachers now feel more supported and management monitoring within the Faculty is more likely to bear fruit than would have been possible in the previously small department.'

Making recommendations

The recommendations section is also brief; it should be very concise and can usually be presented in a simple list format, sometimes with bullet points or numbers. Numbers are probably best avoided unless they do actually represent the order of importance of your recommendations.

Once again, and even more critical here, is to ask yourself for whom the recommendations are intended – colleagues, peers, line supervisors, executives, regional authorities, government ministers? You need to be completely realistic and put forward recommendations for actions which have some chance of being considered and, hopefully, implemented. Thus, recommending a change in national policy is unlikely to be noted, whereas recommending the institution's leadership team to consider a re-appraisal of the company's policy in light of the research findings may have some validity.

Again, each single recommendation needs to be able to be supported by precise evidence in the research when required. Such support is *not* used in the recommendation statement.

Any implementation action arising from a recommendation is likely (although not always) to proceed in small steps to produce effective change. The realistic nature of the changes proposed (mentioned above) should take into account the use of new resources, especially finance, which may be affected by the prevailing economic climate. The more realistic your recommendations are, the more likely your audience is to realise that you and your research are rooted in 'the real world' and are not offering some remote, theoretical study.

One particular recommendation worth considering is the need for further research. As you are not a professional researcher, this will not be seen by the cynical reader as a ploy to obtain further work! Where your research evidence has proved inconclusive or relevant to a particular sample only, a genuine recommendation could be for further research to be undertaken to see whether the results are replicated. In the example given earlier in 'Setting out the conclusions', Phoebe's recommendation was:

> The company should consider commissioning research into the feasibility of such induction programmes for new non-graduate employees having an impact upon staff retention.

 Case example 7.3

Anastasia, a student from Italy, studying in Britain for her Masters in Business Studies, researched the extent to which employees' involvement in the Strategic Plan for the company for which she worked had been effective. Her conclusions showed a mixed report and her recommendations were as follows:

Recommendations

- Those responsible for the final Strategic Plan should indicate at an early stage the form of employees' involvement and the extent to which their views would be noted.
- When the Plan is finished, feedback should be given to all employees concerning the factors which had determined the inclusion or omission of specific employee ideas.

- Employees should organise more formal means for feedback to be given to Senior Managers.
- Employees should meet separately from Senior Managers before the first formal sessions involving proposals.

It is hoped that these recommendations would offer greater opportunities for employee involvement and develop a more positive attitude to what is generally regarded on all sides as a step forward for the company.

Summary of Chapter Seven

This chapter has:

- Suggested the overall structure of the section on presenting and analysing findings
- Described some ways in which quantitative data may be presented
- Described some ways in which qualitative data may be presented
- Given guidance on analysing quantitative data
- Given guidance on analysing qualitative data
- Suggested how to approach analysis of the total data
- Stressed the importance of being self-critical of one's findings
- Proposed how to write 'Conclusions'
- Proposed how 'Recommendations' should be made.

Further reading

Black, T. (1999) *Doing Quantitative Research*. London: Sage.
Denscombe, M. (1998) *The Good Research Guide*. Buckingham: Open University Press.

8

Making the Most of
Available Support

Introduction

After the camaraderie of working in a group during the taught element of your Masters Level programme, moving on to the next phase of carrying out and writing up the research for your Masters Level project can be a solitary activity. It is easy to become isolated as you work on your individual project and this might lead you to exaggerate any potential problems or fail to see potential solutions. It is therefore important that you establish a series of support mechanisms to enable you to complete the process with the minimum amount of disruption and the maximum amount of guidance. A significant person in this process will be your project tutor or supervisor. Different HE institutions use a range of terms to describe the person who will provide you with support during your project. In this chapter, in common with other parts of the book, we will use the term 'tutor' to describe the person providing on-going support and guidance during your project.

In addition to your tutor, other individuals and groups will also have an important role to play in providing you with appropriate support, including: friends and family, peer group, other HE staff and work colleagues. However, whatever the source of support, the main objective for you is to ensure that you have the appropriate level of support, at the right times to ensure success in your Masters Level project.

In this chapter the following topics are considered:

- The role of the tutor
- The range of electronic support that is available
- The importance of peer support

- Getting help from work colleagues
- Practical resource support
- Potential areas of conflict and conflict resolution
- When things go wrong.

Role of the tutor

You will have been allocated a project tutor who has expertise in the subject area you have chosen to investigate, or has more general expertise in the type of research methodology you are planning to use. This person will often be different from the personal tutor you have been given, who has a broader pastoral role and is not directly associated with the project. Your personal tutor will still be able to provide you with pastoral support, but the responsibility for work associated with your project rests firmly with your project tutor. It is important that you recognise this distinction and do not confuse the two very different roles. Your project tutor will have experience of supervising, examining and teaching at Masters Level and has a key role to play in making sure you achieve the best outcome possible.

You may have the opportunity to request a particular member of staff to act as your tutor, but it is more normal practice for the course leader of your Masters Level programme to undertake the allocation of your tutor. The allocation of tutors to individual students is often a complicated logistical exercise; for example, in the authors' institution there are over 600 Masters Level students of leadership and management in a variety of locations in the UK and overseas. You may have established a good working relationship with a member of staff who has taught one of your earlier modules and that person might be your first choice as your project tutor. However, getting the tutor of your choice might not be as easy as you first imagine. Realistically, you should expect to be allocated a suitable tutor with the right skills at the appropriate time in your studies to enable you to commence and to successfully finish your project. At the outset it is reasonable to have a number of general expectations of your tutor:

- That a pattern of regular contact is established
- Positive support is made available
- Feedback and support is provided within an appropriate time frame
- Your tutor establishes clear guidelines and expectation about your progress.

Equally your tutor will have some general expectations of you to:

- Complete tasks on time
- Accept advice and guidance

- Keep in regular contact
- Notify your tutor of changes in your project design.

It is the responsibility of you and your tutor together to find an appropriate level of contact during the preparation of the project. You need to contact your tutor when you have something definite to discuss, ideas to share or work to discuss. Whilst a chat with your tutor can be useful and supportive it is best to identify a definite purpose to your meeting. As a rule of thumb, this meeting could be once a week (maximum) or fortnight (minimum) for full-time students and once a fortnight (maximum) or month (minimum) for part-time students. Unless you are a distance learning student, meetings will usually be face-to-face and last up to one hour. Do not set specific time limits, and aim to achieve particular objectives rather than aiming to fill a set amount of time. A focused meeting lasting 10 minutes can often be more productive than a meeting lasting an hour which has no clear objectives. Remember, much preparatory and actual work can be done through the exchange of emails and attachments and we will return to this in the next section.

Your tutor will give you advice on your research and on preparing your final project and you can expect your tutor to give you specific advice on:

- Developing an appropriate topic area
- Finding literature, but not necessarily recommending specific texts
- Focusing research questions
- Being realistic about scope and timing
- Gaining access
- Ethical issues
- Choosing appropriate methods
- Planning data collection and data analysis
- Writing up
- Submitting the project.

Your tutor is there to guide you through from the start to the finish of your project. However, your tutor cannot carry out your research, undertake analysis or write your project for you, and their role is to provide support and guidance. The research, analysis and writing, with guidance from your tutor, is obviously up to you to complete.

As a starting point your tutor will often ask you to produce a plan for your project. The plan will ask you to identify the research topic, to formulate a limited number of research questions, identify research methods and to develop a time line for the duration of your project. Do not be daunted by this request because the initial plan is a working document and is only intended to get you started. At this stage the most important issues are the topic and what you want to find out (the research questions). Only once you have decided what you want to find out should you go on to decide the methods you will use to find out the information you require.

As you work through your project, the plan will be amended and developed. Each tutor will, within a common framework, have a slightly different way of working which should be tailored to meet your individual needs. If, for example, you are a person who responds well to tight deadlines then it is a good idea to make that clear to your tutor who can respond accordingly. Equally if you respond more positively to a more flexible approach make that clear to your tutor who should respond by establishing more flexible work protocols. You have to arrive at a working arrangement with your tutor that suits both parties. Some tutors may appear to be more dogmatic than others, but the core purpose of your tutor is to make sure that you succeed in your Masters Level project.

The key issue for you is to establish a positive working relationship with your tutor. At the beginning of your project you may feel daunted by your tutor, but the relationship should develop from a teacher–student relationship to one based on two-way communication. Do not be afraid to make your point firmly but politely, and engage in a positive dialogue. Always remember that your tutor is a resource that you are able to draw on and in most cases they will have vast experience of working with students at this level. Do not assume that your tutor will initiate contact, and the responsibility for maintaining contact and establishing clear lines of communication will often rest with you, so be proactive. Be clear and realistic about your expectations, always keep in touch with your tutor and if in doubt do not be afraid to ask your tutor for clarification.

The 'golden rule' is:

> Your tutor is the single most important person you will work with during your Masters Level project. You need to develop a positive and open working relationship with your tutor. Establish clear lines of communication and listen to the advice you are given.

In many HE institutions the project tutor is also responsible for the first marking of your project. If this is the case, advice from your tutor takes on even greater significance, although you should always listen to the advice your tutor gives you, even if they are not directly involved in your final assessment. Even though your tutor should know you and your work well, the final assessment of your project will have to be carried out according to the common assessment criteria that operate on your Masters Level programme. You should make sure you are fully aware of the assessment criteria that relates to your Masters Level programme in your particular HE institution. We will return to the issue of assessment in detail in Chapter Ten.

Electronic support

You may be in a position where you have regular face-to-face contact with your tutor, but this will not be the case for many students who are studying at a distance from their home HE institution. Whatever category you fall into, you will want to make use of electronic communication to keep in touch with your tutor. It may be the major method of contact with your tutor if you are a distance learning student or a student based overseas. Currently we are acting as tutors for a number of overseas based students, and whilst a visit to Brazil or to China would be potentially attractive and useful, it is not a realistic option for a project tutorial. In these cases we have to rely on electronic communication to keep in touch with our Masters Level students. We have learnt from experience, over many years, the advantages and disadvantages of electronic communication methods!

Electronic communication can be used for a variety of purposes, ranging from asking a quick question requiring clarification to sending a draft of your project to your tutor for checking. Your tutor might use electronic communication to make available to you, and to other students, information about new developments in your chosen subject area or details of relevant newly published literature. You might also establish a group discussion with other students to discuss common areas of interest and to share ideas and information.

It is useful for students and tutors to establish a few basic ground rules about the purpose and process of electronic communication before they begin the process:

- Decide on the purpose of electronic communication. Is the purpose to replace face-to-face meetings or is it intended to be used to pass information, submit drafts and to check progress? Will you use electronic communication with your tutor for specific purposes or do you intend to involve a wider group of people in your discussions to share ideas?
- Establish guidelines about response times, and in particular be realistic about your expectations. For example, if you send your tutor a 5,000-word draft you cannot expect an instant response. The tutor will require a reasonable amount of time to read the material you have sent, and bear in mind the tutor might have six other students sending the same amount of material at the time you pressed the send button on your laptop. Equally, a response from your tutor to you about material you sent to your tutor six months earlier will be of little practical use.

- Clarify the groups and individuals who will be involved in any electronic network you set up. Do you intend to establish a support group with other students to share and discuss your ideas or will tutors be involved? The content of a group involving just students might be very different to a group which also has tutors as members.
- Recognise the technical limitations of the equipment you are using and in some cases the technical limitations of your tutor! Remember when dealing with technology that things can and do go wrong, so always ensure you have appropriate back-up to safeguard against the possibility of the loss or corruption of material. If you do not receive a reply from your tutor within an acceptable time period there may be technical problems, so try again!

Electronic support can be quick and, when it works, relatively easy, giving you almost instant access to your tutor or other members of your support network. Once you have established a positive working relationship with your tutor you will soon develop routines relating to electronic communication. You will get to know how quickly you can expect a response to your emails and exactly what is appropriate to send to your tutor. In turn your tutor will use it as an invaluable method to maintain contact with you and as a means to check on your progress. You will also establish routines with other members of your support group about the type of electronic support you can offer each other during the duration of your project. The sharing of information with students in areas such as methodology, access and literature may, in the long run, prove to be invaluable.

You will come to rely on electronic communication as one of your most valuable tools as you complete your Masters Level project. However, for many students, despite the numerous advantages of electronic communication, it cannot replace the personal nature of face-to-face tutorials with your tutor, however sporadic they may be. This is especially true if things go wrong with your project, when the calming words of your tutor, over a cup of coffee, can provide the necessary relief and reassurance to enable you to regroup and carry on. Unfortunately this is not an option for distance learning and international students who will need to make the best possible use of the electronic support that is available to ensure success in their project.

Peer support

Support from fellow students who are working towards the same goal as you will prove invaluable to you as move from the taught element of your course to your individual project. Hopefully you will already have established a network of people, from your Masters Level programme, whom you feel comfortable working with, and who are prepared to share ideas and provide advice.

This sharing process may already have happened in the earlier part of your programme during the taught sessions, but you will need to make sure that this network is maintained as you start to work on your individual project. In the past you will have supported each other on a range of issues, including logistical arrangements, assessment and in some cases understanding of basic topics. Support from your peer group can prove invaluable in:

- *Providing a sounding board for ideas*: It is often a good idea to get feedback from your peers on your choice of topic and your methodology because they can provide you with a different perspective. You should aim to draw on the widest range of advice possible. Do not be afraid to ask for advice and guidance from your peers.
- *Securing access to research data*: Other members of your group might be able to secure access to potential research sites and groups. You may be able to develop reciprocal arrangements that benefit a range of people who are experiencing similar access problems to you.
- *Checking material*: Getting another person to check your work can prove invaluable because they are looking at the material without any of the preconceived ideas you might have. It is always a good idea to get other people to check your use of English, presentation and writing style. This can be especially useful for students who do not have English as a first language. Getting a native speaker to check your work will provide the opportunity to make sure you do not make any basic errors in your use of English or in the presentation of your material.
- *Developing understanding*: You might be having difficulty understanding a concept or even an administrative requirement. It is doubtful that you will be the only person in this situation and making use of peer support might provide you with an easy solution to your problem. It is surprising how many people, even at this level, suffer in silence. Identifying a suitable support group is one way around this type of problem.
- *Extending the range of pastoral support that is available*: Your peers will have had similar experiences to you and may be facing the same problems. The opportunity to share issues is always valuable and sometimes you might just need to moan to someone who understands what you are doing or what you are experiencing. Although you must be careful not to become too negative and you must retain a positive approach to your work.

Establishing a peer support network can play an important part in easing the transition from being a member of a group to working as an individual. However, there are a number of issues that you need to be aware of:

- It can be a formal – with set dates and appropriate venues – or an informal network, where people just meet occasionally when issues occur which might be useful for a few students to talk over together.

- You have to establish a process or forum to set up a network of peer support. It is easy for the group dynamics to get lost as you all go your separate ways and you are no longer meeting on a regular basis. Electronic communication can be useful in establishing a network and your tutor might have a role to play in facilitating peer support for you and your fellow students. Peer support will only happen if you and your colleagues work at establishing a forum.
- Remember you are working alone on your project and whilst co-operation with other students can have obvious benefits you have to do the work. Do not do anything that could lead to you being accused of plagiarism.
- Make sure you feel comfortable about sharing your ideas and plans with other people. Establish trust and be confident that your ideas will not be borrowed by someone else.
- Trust is essential but not only in relation to the sharing of ideas. Your research may involve sensitive or confidential issues and you have to be sure that other people can maintain the confidentiality of your research. There might also be other sensitive pastoral issues and again ensure you trust the people you share your problems with.
- Do not allow advice from your peers to override guidance from other areas. Too often students say they took a particular action because they were advised by other students, for example, 'you have to write a certain number of words in that section'. Check with your tutor and in the published guidelines. Do not always just accept advice and guidance from fellow students at face value.
- Finally, as in many other aspects of life, there is a tendency when a group of people gather together to focus on the negative aspects of the situation. Whilst peer support can be invaluable, remember to remain positive, and do not always focus on the negative.

Work colleagues

If you are a part-time student and are also employed, as you complete your project your work colleagues can also be a valuable source of support. They may give you similar help and advice to that provided by your peer group, but there may be additional particular support that your work colleagues can provide. Your work colleagues will be especially important to you if you are carrying out practitioner research. We discussed the issues relating to this approach in Chapter Six and identified the key benefits that this type of research can bring. The greatest potential advantage is ease of access, and your work colleagues will be instrumental in ensuring your access to the people and documents you need to complete your project.

In addition your work colleagues will be able to act as a sounding board for the work you are proposing to carry out. They will be well placed to comment on your research and your findings. Of course, there may be issues that you have identified, as part of your research, that you may not wish to share with your colleagues and you will have to be sensitive to the practicalities of the situation. However, your work colleagues should be able to give you feedback on what you have written and discovered during your research project. They will also have an important role to play in the implementation of any recommendations you have put forward as part of your project. If you are proposing changes that are going to affect your colleagues and their working practices it is important that they are fully involved in the process. Maintaining communication with your work colleagues for the duration of the project and providing them with regular updates will make implementation of any recommendations you put forward easier. Make sure you involve your work colleagues in what you are doing and keep them informed of the progress you are making. There is nothing to be gained from overt secrecy, so try to maintain open lines of communication with the people you work with.

Your line manager might be of particular importance to you and this is a person whom you will need to involve in the progress of your research. They will obviously be involved in the implementation of any recommendations you make as a consequence of your research project. Your line manager will also be able to be the person who will be able to ensure access and might also be in a position to provide you with additional support. Asking for time off to complete the writing up of your project will be easier if your line manager has been kept informed of what you are doing and they are aware of the positive impact your findings could have on the organisation. The support of your line manager can be significant in easing your progress and is another factor that can ensure your success.

There may also be people in your organisation who have gone through a similar process to the one you are going through as you complete your Masters Level programme. If there are other members of staff who have already completed a Masters Level qualification it is a good idea to talk to them to share ideas. You may be able to build on the work they have already done, but again be careful to avoid any danger of plagiarism. Your work has to be original, but there may be obvious areas of overlap and progression that will provide valuable opportunities for your particular project. At the very least, talking to people who have completed a similar programme to you will provide you with access to someone who has experienced the practical problems of studying part-time whilst working full- or part-time. Talking to someone who has been through a similar process might save you a large amount of time and wasted effort because they can provide you with valuable advice and guidance.

Practical resource support

As you have progressed through your Masters Level programme you will have been provided with access to a number of resources. Taking advantage of the support provided by the range of resources available to you will make your research easier to complete. You should take every opportunity to utilise the range of support available to you and remember it is designed to make your project easier to complete. You will have paid a large amount in tuition fees and it is reasonable to expect that appropriate practical resources are provided to enable you to carry out your research effectively and efficiently. Within your HE institution there is likely to be a range of resource support available:

- *Online materials*: Your HE institution and your own department is likely to have a range of materials available online including: study skills information, academic writing guidance, assessment criteria, presentation guidelines and specific academic materials.
- *Library*: You will already be familiar with the facilities available in your library, but extra help might be available to support you in your project. Check to see if there is a dedicated member of staff who is able to provide you with support in areas such as your literature search and with locating previous completed projects in your subject area.
- *Subject staff*: There may be other members of staff, in addition to your tutor, who have particular subject expertise and who may be able to provide you with additional support. However, if you are going to contact other members of staff keep your tutor informed of what you are doing. There is a danger that you may alienate people if you do not manage this process properly!
- *Specific study skills support or checking service*: Many HE institutions have dedicated members of staff who will provide you with specific advice about study skills and academic writing. If English is not your native language some HE institutions offer an English language checking service to correct your use of English and to support you in developing a good writing style. Remember that in both cases the support is available to check on the quality of your written work, not on the academic content.
- *Welfare services*: A range of support systems will be in place to provide you with pastoral support if you have personal or medical problems. There will be a full counselling service to provide advice and support on personal problems. If you have health problems make sure you maintain proper records to present to your tutor who may have to argue your case to the examination board. There will also be additional academic support available if you encounter issues that cannot be dealt with by your project tutor or if the relationship with your tutor breaks down.
- *Technical support*: There may be technicians who can provide access and guidance to particular equipment, for example recording equipment for interviews or video. Technical staff may also be available to assist you in establishing communication with other students.

We have already pointed out the importance of support from work colleagues. If you are working and studying part-time, in addition to the resource support provided by your HE institution, you may have support available in your employing organisation:

- *Library*: Your organisation might have a library which can provide additional materials and also a member of staff who can provide additional assistance in areas such as your literature search. If you are carrying out practitioner research your organisation's library might have access to specific technical documents that are not widely available elsewhere.
- *IT support*: You may have dedicated IT support staff within your organisation who can offer specific guidance on IT hardware and software. They may be able to provide advice about techniques and approaches that save you time and a great deal of effort.
- *Technical support*: Your own organisation might have similar, or in some cases better, equipment available for you to use to gather data.
- *Secretarial support*: You may be in the fortunate position that you have access to secretarial support who can provide help in areas such as transcription of interviews or even something as mundane as photocopying.

Conflict resolution

We do not want to overestimate the significance of this area because in our experience it is very unusual for major conflicts to happen as students complete their project. Provided you follow our guidance to maintaining effective communication and keep people informed of what you are doing in your project, conflict should not arise. However, we need to consider the issues that might cause conflict and the procedures for dealing with it.

A first obvious source of conflict might be with your tutor. If differences do develop it is usually because either you or your tutor are not doing what has been previously agreed. As we outlined earlier in the chapter both you and your tutor should have clear expectations and these should be set out early in the relationship. For instance, it is reasonable to point out to your tutor if you feel they are taking too long to respond to questions you are asking or in providing a commentary on written work you have submitted. However, there may be good reasons for the delay and you need to communicate your concerns clearly. Be assured that if you are not keeping to your part of the agreement your tutor will soon let you know!

There may be very rare occasions when a student and tutor relationship breaks down completely and there will be set procedures in your HE institution to deal with this eventuality. Given the pressures students and tutors are often working under a total breakdown of the relationship can occur, but it is extremely unusual for this to happen. Remember you do not have to like your tutor, but it helps! What you require is a positive working relationship which enables you to achieve your goal of successfully finishing your Masters Level project. If you have major problems with your tutor, you should normally contact your course leader in the first instance. If you are still not satisfied with supervision arrangements, usually you should contact the Director of Postgraduate Taught Courses in your HE institution. However, in the vast majority of cases where conflict arises a simple conversation can often lead to an amicable agreement being reached.

Another possible area of conflict could be between you and your research subjects or any organisation you are working in to collect data. We have discussed the research approaches you should adopt and more particularly the ethical guidelines you should follow in Chapters Five and Six. You have to follow agreed principles and adhere to the guidelines you have set out when you commenced the research project. Unfortunately, if your research starts to unravel and there is major conflict between you and the organisation or individual research subjects, you have no choice but to withdraw and make a fresh start. Again this should only happen in extreme circumstances and you must make every effort to maintain good relations with your research subjects.

When we discussed practitioner research in Chapter Six we identified the possible pitfalls of this approach because of a potential conflict of interest. You will need to make sure you do not do anything to jeopardise your access, whilst at the same time making sure your research is honest and realistic. You do not want to find yourself in a situation where you are in conflict with your employer, so make sure you conform to the guidelines you agreed at the outset. If you do find yourself in conflict with your employer, make sure you keep your tutor involved in the process, they may be able to provide invaluable advice and suggest a solution to the problem.

In Chapter Ten we will look at a range of issues relating to the final assessment of your project. The final assessment of your project is another potential area of conflict because you may be dissatisfied with the mark and grade you are awarded after you have submitted your project. If there are mitigating circumstances that can be used to explain what you consider to be your relatively poor performance they should be made known to your tutor. Your HE institution will have detailed guidelines on the process you have to follow if you are dissatisfied with your final grade and any appeals procedure that you are able to access. You may need to make use of the additional academic support provided by your HE institution if you find yourself having to go through the appeal process.

Ideally you do not want to find yourself in a situation where conflict might arise. Avoiding conflict is of crucial importance and an integral part of this is effective communication with the various stakeholders you work with during your project. The identification of clear guidelines and expectations will enable you to manage the project with the minimum amount of upset. There is nothing wrong with you knowing and identifying your rights as a student, but always remember that you also have responsibilities. There will be occasions when you have to compromise, but remember that your prime objective is successful completion of your Masters Level project.

The 'golden rule' here is:

> With rights come responsibilities. Treat other stakeholders as you would expect to be treated and always keep lines of communication open.

When things go wrong

In this chapter we have outlined a number of strategies to ensure that you make the most of the available support, but there may be occasions when even this is not enough to prevent problems arising. You may experience personal or health problems that result in you having to request an extension beyond your original submission date. You should only do this as a last resort, but you should not view it as a weakness or sign of failure. There will be set procedures in place within your own HE institution that you will have to follow in order to obtain an extension. In most cases you will have to submit a written request for an extension and it can only be granted by a senior member of staff – usually your project tutor does not have the authority to grant long-term extensions. Many HE institutions have a pro forma that you have to complete to get an extension and you will normally need the support of your tutor who should be kept informed of your problems.

You will not have to go into great detail about your personal circumstances to get an extension but you will have to give some indication of the problem you are facing. If there are medical reasons for your request for an extension you may be asked to provide supporting documentation from your doctor. The granting of an extension is not normally viewed as a problem by the HE institution, but there has to be a legitimate reason for your request. Feeling tired or being busy is not usually considered to be sufficient justifications for an extension to the amount of time allowed to complete your project. However, health and personal issues will be viewed sympathetically, and you can, in extreme cases, be granted up to 12 months' additional time to complete your project. Remember, your research project is not as important as your health or personal well-being, so do not be afraid to ask for help and guidance and if you need an extension to your studies. Provided you complete your project in the extended allocated time period your overall mark and grade should not be reduced. However, it is important that you resume your studies as soon as possible to minimise the impact on your own work and to maintain momentum.

Summary of Chapter Eight

This chapter has:

- Explained the key role of the tutor in providing support
- Described the range and purpose of electronic support that is likely to be available
- Discussed the importance of peer support as you progress through your project
- Explained the importance of getting help from your work colleagues
- Outlined the range of practical resource support that is available to you
- Discussed potential areas of conflict and how they can be resolved
- Outlined the procedures if things go wrong and if you need to request an extension.

Further reading

Potter, S. (2006) *Doing Postgraduate Research.* London: Sage.
Wellington, J. (2010) *Making Supervision Work for You: A Student's Guide.* London: Sage.

9

Writing Up

Introduction

When all the research has been completed and recorded, the assessment of your work and the award of your Masters Degree depends ultimately on what you submit. The form in which your report is made is therefore crucial. This chapter deals with the subject of how that report is written, in terms of style and format. Whether you write up each section as it is completed, or save all the writing up until the end, the issues are the same. This chapter considers the following:

- The order in which the project is written
- What overall style should be used
- Writing in a language other than your native one
- Avoiding plagiarism
- Using references correctly and compiling the bibliography
- Formatting
- The use of appendices
- Checking your work
- Writing acknowledgements
- Writing the abstract.

The order in which your project is written

Considering that the structure of the project was given clearly in Chapter Two, this may seem an odd thing to consider. However, it is a fact that most people do not start at the beginning and proceed logically through to the end.

Many established academic writers, for example, write the Introduction last of all! Also many people prefer to write what they feel are the easiest sections first. Some sections such as the Literature Review (Chapter Three) or the Presentation of Findings (in Chapter Seven) are free standing and can be written separately then inserted in the correct place in the final report. Thus, you should begin where *you* feel most comfortable and work from there, taking into account all the points that are made in this chapter.

The crucial thing is that you write regularly – that way, you develop the writing habit. All professional writers tell us that, whatever the topic, you need to develop this habit and not wait for inspiration to come. Producing some writing leads to more writing! Zerubavel (1999) neatly calls this 'The clockwork muse'.

The style of writing to be used

The crucial issue for any writer in considering *how* something is written is to address the question of readership or audience. 'For whom am I writing?' is the first question for any writer. In the case of your writing your leadership project or dissertation, this is relatively straightforward: you are writing primarily for your academic assessors as they will make the judgement on your work and grade or evaluate it accordingly. The next chapter, Chapter Ten, examines this issue of assessment in detail. However, in many cases, Masters students are also presenting the work for their sponsors or employers and the work needs to be accessible to these also. It is possible that you may ask 'What about me? Am I not also writing for myself? It is my work!' In one sense the answer is 'not directly', but as Briggs (2002: 285) expresses it:

> Your own opinion – in the form of your own interests, ethics and priorities – will shape the whole of your research: it will guide you in choosing what questions to ask, what literature to read, what methodology to adopt, what factors to analyse in your data and what importance to place upon your findings.

In other words, it is all yours – but it has to be expressed in a particular way and we need to consider what features of an appropriate style of writing should be used.

Use the past tense

This is important because you are essentially writing a report on the work that has been carried out. You may need to do some amending in writing up because in your proposal and probably in early drafts of some sections, such as methodology, you will have used the future tense in saying what you intend to do. All these need to be altered so that the whole project is in the past tense – with just three exceptions.

(i) The first is any statement in the Introduction about yourself. For example, 'The researcher is a manager of …' , 'The writer works as a Head of Department in …'
(ii) The second is obviously in quotations from other writers
(iii) The third is, occasionally, when you make a statement about some general principle that is true all of the time, for example 'Motivating staff is seen as a key responsibility of managers'.

Write in the third person (or passive or indirect voice)

Morrison (2002: 25) claims that this recommendation of the use of third person is an indication of how far positivist approaches to research have become the norm. It is true that in some kinds of ethnographic research where a narrative approach is used, the use of the first person 'I' and 'We' can be appropriate. If you think this applies to you, consult your project or supervising tutor. Nevertheless, it is true that the third person will be the most appropriate for 95% of projects or dissertations submitted at Masters Level. One minor exception to this rule can again be in the 'Introduction' where you introduce yourself and your context. Even here, many students prefer to use 'the writer' or 'the researcher' – for example, 'The writer [or researcher] is a Head of Department in a secondary school …'. This helps you to get into the habit of using the third person throughout and helps to prevent you falling back into the use of 'I' in the Methodology section. 'A random sampling process was chosen as the most appropriate because…' should always be written – rather than 'I chose random sampling as the most appropriate method because …'.

The huge and overriding advantage of using the third person is the *objectivity* that it brings to the whole process. You are presenting your research and its findings in an unbiased way, standing back from any emotions you might have about them, in order to seek the truth. This style in no way means your language is stilted or you are less creative. What it does is eliminate the personality of the individual carrying out the research and allows the reader to focus on the research itself without being sidetracked into wondering about the writer as a person. Your style is about engaging the reader, and your individuality will still come through. This is best illustrated by making the point that if two different students carried out the same research, with the same findings, the actual reports would be different! The individuality of the writer makes this the case. A number of Masters students are practitioners who have not written anything like an assignment or project for many years before joining the programme. They will inevitably have patterns of writing which have a habit of entering their work. Although practice will have been gained through writing earlier assignments, it is worth noting some of the further practical points to be used and avoided.

Use formal language and write correctly

Again, this in no way means using a stilted style, but this is an 'official', formal report and a colloquial style is inappropriate. With the obvious exception of quotations from another person or writer, the following should be noted:

(i) Avoid slang and colloquialisms: 'The school chosen was a top notch one', 'the manager was a whiz kid …'.

(ii) Write out all in full: 'Do not' (not 'don't'), they are (not 'they're'), 'they will' (not 'they'll'), and so on. These are speech patterns and not appropriate here.

(iii) Keep jargon to an absolute minimum: Jargon can be useful within a specific professional context because it can be a convenient method of describing concepts in that world. But it should be used sparingly, otherwise it can assume an importance beyond that which it actually has. It can also make you appear as if you are showing off!

(iv) Use abbreviations correctly: This means that the first time a phrase with a commonly accepted abbreviation occurs, write it out in full, putting the abbreviation in brackets afterwards. For example, '… the Head of Department (HOD) …' or 'Human Resource Management (HRM)'. Thereafter, the abbreviation will suffice. If a large number of abbreviations are used, you may wish to include a 'Glossary of Terms' in your final project report version – as we have done in this book. You should note that different terminologies may exist for what is basically the same thing in different countries, and, occasionally, the same initials mean different things. For example, 'SBM' stood for 'school-based management' in England in the 1990s, whilst 'SBM' stood for 'site-based management' in Canada, Australia and New Zealand – and still does.

(v) Keep the language simple: Try to avoid unnecessary wording such as 'meet up with' for 'meet', 'complexity and difficulty in being understood' for 'complexity'. Try to avoid clichés and phrases which have become rather formulaic through over-use. Do not write 'this moment in time', when you mean 'now' or 'currently'. Phrases in 'management-speak', such as 'thinking outside the box' or 'blue skies thinking' are fast becoming clichés, so think carefully when tempted to use them.

(vi) Avoid biased language: Language constantly changes and words or phrases which were once acceptable can sometimes no longer be so. This is particularly true in terms of gender. Female forms of words such as actress, waitress, policewoman, headmistress, have mostly disappeared so that, regardless of gender, waiters, actors, police officers, headteachers are the relevant terms, as are nurses and doctors. A difficulty sometimes arises over a phrase which is needed to refer to 'him or her' when a neutral phrase is needed. Although '(s)he' is sometimes used, many find this an ugly phrase and, if possible, try to simply use the term for the role, as above, for example, 'The principal said ...', 'The manager believed ...'. Similarly, ageism and racism need to be avoided in the language, however inadvertently these may occur. The term 'old age pensioners' is never used in the UK now. 'Senior citizens' would be correct or simply 'pensioners' when referring to anyone actually receiving a pension.

(vii) Use quotations effectively: As you notice above, we have referred to the use of quotations as the exceptions to your normal rules of writing, because these display the actual words used by the person quoted. Interviewees' quotations will contain certain speech patterns, therefore, and may well use colloquialisms or clichés. If this is what is actually said, you must quote it. As we noted in Chapter Seven, quotations enliven and 'make real' research findings. If a quotation in writing (for example, in a questionnaire 'other remarks' return) actually misuses a word, there is an accepted method of recording this. For example, 'The manager lords [sic] his employees regularly'. The respondent means 'lauds' but has misused the word. By putting [sic] as indicated, you shows that it is an exact quote but that you are aware of the error!

(viii) Write clearly: Finally, we cannot stress too strongly the importance of writing with correct:

- Spelling
- Punctuation
- Grammar.

If you are not naturally a good speller, by all means use a computer's spell check, but remember they are not infallible as they generally fail to take account of the context of a word. They also often use Americanisms! Remember things such as, 'practice' is the noun, 'practise' the verb, as with 'advice' and 'advise'; the two 'a's in 'separate' separate the two 'e's; and 'discrete' and 'discreet' have quite different meanings! These are but a few of countless examples of common errors.

In punctuation, some frequently found errors relate to the use of semi-colons. The easiest rule for a semi-colon is to use it rather like a full stop, but between sentences that are closely linked. Also in punctuation, one of the commonest errors lies in the use of the apostrophe, which indicates possession not number – i.e. it should not be placed before an 's' in the case of a plural noun. A frequent cause of error is the case of 'its', which is the possessive form, meaning 'belonging to it' (as with 'hers' or 'yours'), as opposed to 'it's' which is a contraction of 'it is'. When an abbreviation plural is required, no apostrophe is used such as 'LAs' whereas 'the LA's use of inspection services ...' refers to a single authority.

In grammar, the commonest error we see is the failure of the verb to agree with the subject of a sentence, especially when they are separated by a phrase or clause. For example, 'The number of respondents, although slightly below expectation, were judged to be sufficient to ...'. This is wrong as 'number' is singular and it should be 'The number ... was judged ...'.

These are but a few of the slips that do occur – an exhaustive list would occupy a chapter! Simple guides to writing good English do exist and it may well be worth investing in one if you are not confident of your use of language. You need to (a) take care, and (b) get someone else to check – especially if English is not your first language.

It may be worth commenting on approaches to two particular sections – the beginning and the end. In the opening paragraph, you need to capture the reader's attention so think hard about that. The best way to establish your style is not to put off the writing but to get started! The final paragraph of the whole project may stay in the reader's mind. Try to end with a flourish, not a bland statement and certainly not with a reference!

 Case example 9.1

Isabella was the Head of Department of a beautician and hairdressing section of a Further Education College in the South of England. Her project for her Masters Degree was research into the impact of the leader as role model on staff motivation. Here are the opening sentences of her Introduction:

'As someone who has always been interested in why people do what they do and why people behave differently, the writer did not find it difficult to decide that some aspect of motivation would be central to the research needed for her final project. Since becoming head of a department with 10 staff in a Further Education College with particular responsibility for courses for young adults, aged 17–22 years, the writer has had opportunity to consider the question of the extent to which a leader may motivate staff through being a role model to staff ...'

At the end of the whole work, in her final paragraph Isabella 'rounded off' her project with the following final sentence.

'These recommendations are ones that it is to be hoped the College will consider carefully and possibly implement. In any case, what the writer has gained from carrying out the research in terms of understanding the impact of personal leadership on staff motivation will serve her well as she continues to develop, personally and professionally.'

Writing in a language other than your native tongue

The first language of the authors of this book is English and we are well aware of the difficulties that we experience in trying to express certain ideas or describe certain situations in our 'other' languages, such as French or Greek! We have nothing but admiration for those of you writing your project in what is to you a second language. You will probably have already taken a language proficiency or competence test to ensure you have the essential fluency to undertake the programme, but it is still a great undertaking when you come to write your major piece of work. Firstly, note everything that has been said to date in this chapter, including the comments on correctness of writing. Secondly, you need to double and if necessary treble check your work, paying special attention to sentence construction. Thirdly, it is essential that someone else with a good command of English reads your work, not to comment on the content but to see if it reads well and if it expresses what you want it to say. As noted with spell checks (above), use English rather than Americanised spelling, and, if in doubt, ask and check again. As the chapter on assessment (Chapter Ten) shows, the presentation of your work can, for some candidates, make the difference between passing and failing.

Flowerdew (1999) found that Hong Kong Chinese students writing in English found the Discussion sections of theses much more difficult than the reporting and descriptive sections, so it may be worth paying special attention to such parts of your work. Partridge and Starfield (2007: 12) describe how, compared with some languages such as Japanese which are 'reader-responsible', English as a language is 'writer-responsible'. In other words, it is very much down to the writer to make the sense of their text clear to the reader. This, therefore, is confirmation of how important it is to have your work checked for clarity of meaning.

Avoiding plagiarism

Plagiarism is now regarded as one of the most serious offences for students attempting to gain awards, and there is international concern about it and a general agreement that anyone guilty of it should not be granted an award. Additionally, the plagiarist could be subject to legal action from the person or publishers whose work has been plagiarised. This problem has greatly increased since the use of the internet became widespread. It is therefore of the utmost importance that you make every possible attempt to avoid it, however accidentally you may claim that it has occurred. The fact that the plagiarism was unintentional will probably not be enough to save your work from being failed. Firstly, therefore, we need to be clear what constitutes plagiarism. Quite simply, it is using other people's words (or figures, drawings or diagrams) without acknowledging their source, thereby presenting the work as if it were your own. At the very least, students are normally asked to sign a statement, saying that they have not used other people's work without acknowledgement or without their consent. Students found guilty of plagiarism can be graded as failures or dismissed from a course. To avoid any risk of unintentional plagiarism, you should keep a careful note of every single piece of literature or information you use as you proceed. You will probably discard several eventually but it is better to have the note just in case. As Denscombe (2002: 59) points out:

> Unless researchers are very careful to keep precise notes during their reading of the various sources, there is a danger that quotes from the original might get lost among the other notes kept by the researcher, so that, when it comes to writing up the research, the quotes are inadvertently and unintentionally included as though they were the researcher's own words.

Our 'golden rule' therefore is:

To avoid unintentional plagiarism, keep a careful record of EVERYTHING you use as a source.

What happens if you wish to use a phrase or sentence that you know belongs to someone else, but you just cannot remember or find the source? Most of us have phrases in our heads, after all, that we know we heard somewhere but we cannot remember where or from whom. When this happens, and you feel the use of the words is essential, you need to put in the quotation and put in brackets after it (*source unknown*). We would not recommend doing this more than once in the whole of your project.

In the next section we deal with how to give references to sources, but you should also note that if you submit a large excerpt from a previous one of your own assignments, this can be seen as falsely claiming it as new work so restrict use of your own previous assignments to brief quotations, fully referenced. The copying of another student's work is similarly viewed as plagiarism.

The use of the web is particularly fraught with potential problems. Not all work found on the web is sourced but this does not mean it is not someone's work or property, so be sure to be clear about this. Wholesale copying from the web is undoubtedly the biggest source of plagiarism today.

Infringing copyright is also illegal, so if, for example, you decide to use an established tool that someone else devised in methodological research (and there are a number of these in the leadership and management field) ensure you state this clearly in your work. Sometimes, you may adjust a diagnostic tool or a diagram to suit your own research purposes, in which case it is crucial that you write this after the model: for example 'Adapted from Belbin (1981)'.

What about sharing work with another student? Unless specific permission has been granted by the institution for a joint submission, the final project must be your individual work. Of course, you will debate and discuss with colleagues on the course and probably at work, but the written work must be yours. It is not impossible for two students on the same Masters programme who are researching similar areas to sit down together and work out appropriate questionnaires for example. This is all good intellectual discourse, but the actual process of research must be separate.

Finally, while plagiarism and copyright raise issues of intellectual property, you may need to check about the actual ownership of your final project or dissertation. In many cases, where sponsors or employees have paid for you to follow the programme and carry out the research, they often, not undeservedly, regard the final report as their property. You would be well advised to check. However, the Masters Degree is yours personally!

A cautionary note for those writing in English as a second language is that a lack of proficiency in language skills is seen by some as a reason for accidental plagiarism, rather than unawareness of its unacceptability as a practice. Thus, all we mentioned in the above section about writing in a language other than your native one applies very strongly here also.

Using references correctly and compiling the bibliography

When assessments are made of the presentational aspect of students' work at Masters Level (see Chapter Ten), we have found that more marks are likely to be lost through incorrect referencing or mistakes in the bibliography than in any other area. Having done several written assignments using referencing already, you should, in theory, be adept at this by the stage of the final project. However, our experience has shown us that this is often not so! Bad habits persist and it is imperative that these are eradicated in your final writing up. We therefore remind you of the basic rules, using the Harvard system of referencing. It is the system we use in this book. (You should ensure that you use the correct system of referencing as specified by your own HE institution, just in case it uses a convention other than the Harvard system.)

(i) Referring to a book author or co-authors in a general sense:

> In education, the importance of staff other than teachers has increased significantly since the later years of the twentieth century (Bush and Middlewood, 2005).

In the Bibliography, this reference would appear as:

Bush, T. and Middlewood, D. (2005) Leading and Managing People in Education. London: Sage.

(Note that italicising can be used instead of underlining here. The crucial point is to be consistent throughout the Bibliography.)

(ii) Referring to a book by three or more co-authors:

> The increased focus on actual learning in education institutions owing to greater understanding of how people learn is shown in the texts about learning schools (Middlewood et al., 2005).

In the Bibliography, this reference would appear as:

Middlewood, D., Parker R. and Beere, J. (2005) Creating a Learning School. London: Paul Chapman Publishing.

(iii) Referring to a specific quote by a book author or authors:

> In looking at the future of leadership development, Bush (2008: 137) suggests that 'leadership preparation is no longer an optional activity'.

(Note that the specific page number is required for a specific quote. Where the quotation is a long one, that is more than a single sentence, the whole quote should be indented.)

> As Bush stated:

> The most successful adult learning appears to grow from the identification of personalised learning needs. However, individualised learning is difficult to organise and can be expensive to deliver. (Bush, 2005: 127)

(Note: the page number(s) should appear after the date in the text.)

(iv) Referring to a chapter by an author in an edited volume: Here, the chapter's author (or authors) is referred to in the main text and the author(s) and the editors in the Bibliography.

> Caldwell (2002) summarised the situation concerning self-managing institutions at the beginning of the twenty first century.

In the Bibliography, this would appear as:

Caldwell, B. (2002) 'Autonomy and Self-Management: Concepts and Evidence', in T. Bush and L. Bell (eds) The Principles and Practice of Educational Management. London: Sage.

(Note that in some publications, more than one of an author's initials may be used and in the example above, editors' initials precede the surname.)

(v)   Referring to a journal article:

Hammond et al. (1998) summarised many of the issues involved in decision-making.

In the Bibliography, this would appear as:

Hammond, J., Keeney, R. and Raiffa, H. (1998) 'The Hidden Traps in Decision Making', <u>Harvard Business Review</u>, 77(4): 47–58.

(vi) You can reference your own previous work by simply using your surname and date in the normal way, with the title in the Bibliography.

(vii) Referring to an indirect source:

Where you locate a quotation used by an author and are unable to locate the original source, you use 'cited in'.

Smith (1997), cited in Adams (2004: 63) points out that staff motivation is 'mysterious and multifarious'.

(viii) Your Bibliography of course is arranged by alphabetical order of authors' surnames.

Where the same author occurs several times, his or her publications are placed strictly in order of date of publication, the oldest first. Where the same author has two or more publications in the same year, you designate each one (a) (b) (c), etc. in the order they appear in your text, then list them in your bibliography accordingly as:

Smith, L. (2003a) _____
Smith, L. (2003b) _____
Smith, L. (2003c) _____

Where the author has published singly, and also co-authored with others, the order is: single named books first, co-authored (with one) next, and with more than one after that – all regardless of date. For example:

Jones, P. (2004) _____
Jones, P. and Smith, L. (2003) _____
Jones, P. and Williams G. (2001) _____
Jones, P., Smith, L. and Williams G. (2000) _____

You may also wish to reference material you have found on the internet. The precise conventions for doing this are not yet fixed, but the system we recommend is as follows. Note that these references indicate the date you accessed the source. Material on the internet tends to be temporary rather than permanent and can often be undated. It is important therefore to place it in time.

For an online journal article:

> Medwell, J. (2000) 'Teachers Learning to use the Internet: Some Insights from the United Kingdom Experience', Reading Online (Online Journal). Available at: www.readingonline.org/international/medwell (Accessed on 12 January 2008).

For a website:

> Wray, D. (undated) 'Literacy Across the World' (website). Available at www.warwick.ac.uk/staff/D.J.Wray.html (Accessed on 12 January 2009).

For a section of a website:

> Wray, D. (undated) 'An Approach to Standard English' (Online article). Available at: www.warwick.ac.uk/staff/D.J.Wray/Standeng.html (Accessed on 12 January 2009).

For a contribution to a discussion group:

> Rog, L. (17 January 2000) 'Excellent Reading Instruction' (Contribution to the RTeacher discussion group RTEACHER@LISTSERV.SYR.EDU). Available at Listserv.syr.edu/archives/rteacher.html (Accessed on 12 January 2006).

(ix)   As you have seen, there are many conventions to observe. Some others are:

- Generally, do not use titles such as 'Doctor' or 'Professor'. Even with public figures such as Government ministers, it is preferable to use the role or post, not the individual's name.
- Do not use footnotes. Those with a scientific background sometimes have to adjust to this, because footnotes are common in specific scientific or technical journals. If a technical or foreign word needs to be explained either put the explanation in brackets after the word or use an asterisk and put an explanation at the end of the section.
- Two Latin abbreviations may be useful:

  op. cit. – means 'the work previously cited' and can be used to avoid constant repetition of the same citation details.
  ibid. – means 'the same' and can be used for the source of a quote if it follows a previous one without any other source used in between.

Finally, you should note that lengthy lists of references in brackets after a point is made do not impress assessors! The key is the appropriate use of sources, accurately referenced.

Formatting your work

Here, the main advice we can give is to study carefully the specific instructions given by the HE institution to whom you are submitting your work. Although requirements are similar across HE institutions, you need to be sure of the exact requirements. For instance, details about font size and margins will be specified.

Your final piece of work should:

- Be doubled spaced
- Be presented on one side of the paper only
- Start each new *major* section on a new page (it is very bad practice to put a section title at the bottom of a page, for example)
- Have consistency of headings, with particular fonts for major or minor headings
- Have a title page at the top of your work. This should have:

  o The title of the work
  o The degree for which it is submitted
  o The name of the HE institution
  o Your name
  o The date of submission (month and year only).

- Include a brief Acknowledgments section. Normally a single paragraph, this enables you to thank those who have helped you complete the work, such as tutor, colleague(s), sponsor, partner, family. This can be included on a separate sheet after the title page before the list of contents
- Include a Contents page. Obviously, this cannot be done in full until your final printing. It is not necessary to include every single sub-section in the contents, but you must show the pages for the Bibliography and Appendices.

Appendices

When a project or dissertation is submitted which is much heavier and thicker than others, assessors are almost certain that the reason is too many appendices have been included. There is no extra credit for this!

There are some things that *must* be included in your appendices. These are the final versions of your research methodological instruments, such as questionnaire(s), interview schedule(s), observation schedule(s). These need to be listed separately, for example:

Appendices:

A. Observation schedule for staff meeting
B. Semi-structured interview schedule for managers
C. Questionnaire for clerical staff

Do not forget to refer to them in the main text in your methodology section for example, after describing piloting, and mentioning changes made: '(See Appendix A for copy of final version of observation schedule)'.

Note that some institutions require you to include the completed ethical approval form in the appendices.

There are no other compulsory appendices contents. The basic rule is that you should only include something without which the reader will not be able to make sense of as part of the main text. Just because you refer to a company's 'Corporate Plan' in the text, this does not mean you have to put a copy of this Plan into an appendix. However, if you go into some detail and are clear that further detail will just mean copying the document, and if it is the case that knowledge of this detail is important to understanding your points, then include the Plan in an appendix, or if it is a lengthy document, include the relevant section(s). Selecting relevant sections from the relevant document(s) is by far the most appropriate course of action if you are including documents referred to.

Checking your work

One always feels great sympathy for those students whose submissions fall just short of a Pass or are just a mark or two below a grade borderline. However, the authors admit more to irritation in those cases where those few marks could so easily have been gained through checking their work carefully, especially as those students will have been told to do just that! The very last thing, therefore, that you need to do before submitting your work is to check it – and double check it! Far too many marks are lost because of failure to carry out a thorough review of the whole piece. Some writers like to check carefully at the end of each section; others prefer to check everything right at the end. Ideally, do both. However, a final check is essential in any case. We suggest that having another person read through the work, not examining content but concentrating on spotting errors, is the best way. Proof-reading your own work is notoriously difficult and even the very best professional writers miss their own errors. To have someone who will query, 'Is this how you spell...?' or 'What do you mean by this?' is invaluable.

We suggest you make a checklist for yourself and this other person. It perhaps should include:

- Title page – are all details included?
- Contents page – are page numbers correct? Appendices included?
- Abstract – is it included and of correct length?
- Acknowledgements included and complete?
- Format – margins and font are all correct as per instructions? Does each major section begin on a new page?

- Headings – are they consistent?
- References – all correct? Dates and page numbers included?
- Bibliography – correct order?
- Spelling – correction and consistency?
- Punctuation and paragraphing
- Have the verbs been changed to past tense from earlier proposals?
- Figures – are they correctly labelled and numbered?

These elementary checks do not take as long as the length of this list might suggest. The time spent is well worth it in terms of saving marks lost!

Writing the acknowledgements

This brief section is seen as an essential courtesy in that it thanks those who have helped you in your completion of the project.

A useful division can be into thanking those who provided:

- Academic assistance
- Resources (including any financial help)
- Participation in the project
- Moral support.

And including:

- Personal acceptance of responsibility for any errors
- Any personal dedication.

(Based on Hyland, 2004; Partridge and Starfield, 2007)

Writing the abstract

An abstract is a concise summary of the completed work. Usually of between 300 and 400 words (the length is sometimes specified by the individual institution) and can be a single paragraph or, at the most, two to three very brief paragraphs. It is appropriate that we deal with this last because writing the abstract is the very last piece of writing you do. You cannot after all write it until all the work is completed.

Economy of words is more important than ever here but you must still use complete sentences and follow the same rules for style described earlier. Write it in the past tense and make no specific references to particular aspects in the work, such as a figure or table.

You should include brief statements on:

- The purpose of the work
- Its significance, possibly mentioning 'previous literature' but, as above, no specific references
- The methodology and sampling used – without detailed numbers
- The findings in broad terms
- The conclusions.

Doing a draft of your abstract first is crucial because of the economy of words needed. You may well need to edit your first draft to bring it to the correct length. Head the sheet simply 'Abstract' and be ready to insert it in your work as a separate page. Do not put your name at the end of the abstract. We give two examples below, one from Elliot working in education, the second from Jo working in a business context.

 Case example 9.2

Abstract

This dissertation examined the impact of the external Quality Assurance Service (QAS) on primary schools in a small African Island nation state. The QAS's purpose is both to support these schools and also hold them accountable for educational standards. A multiple case study of three particular schools on the same island was used.

A review of the literature suggested that such external services in various countries served different purposes, with a much greater emphasis generally upon monitoring and accountability than upon support, this often being offered by a different localised agency.

The methodology employed involved a survey of all teaching staff in these schools, using a questionnaire, semi-structured interviews with a stratified sample of those staff and also with three members of the QAS team linked with the schools. Additionally, documentary analysis of QAS schedules and the schools' development plans were used.

The analysis of the data showed that whilst many staff felt the QAS was supportive, a number were unsure how its processes impacted on their accountability, a view shared by some of the QAS team. The dissertation concludes that greater clarity of the accountability process of the QAS would lead to greater impact.

Case example 9.3

Abstract

This project set out to investigate the impact upon the organisational culture of a female senior manager since her appointment to the leadership of a previously all-male unit of a medium-sized company. The researcher was granted access to the unit and to all staff in order to gain an initial impression of the culture before and since the senior manager's appointment.

The Literature Review revealed general agreement over the meaning of organisational culture but divergent views on the impact of leadership upon it, ranging from very little impact to, at worse, destructive.

The research was carried out using semi-structured interviews with all the existing staff and with the senior manager at the start of her taking up the post, and at the end of the six-month research period. Careful analysis was also made of a wide range of documentation over this period, exploring language and style especially.

The data analysis suggested that, whilst some changes had occurred which a majority of males felt was positive, a minority was clear that their original views opposing the appointment were justified. The leader's strategy of adjusting organisational structure and making minor changes in approach was, in her view, having an impact.

The study found that, as much literature suggested, cultural change is gradual and it was possibly fortunate that a general background of economic stability existed at this time, so that a pressure on performance did not exert undue clamour for hurried change.

Note on leadership and management

You will have noticed that virtually everything in this chapter on writing up could be applied to most subjects submitted at Masters Level, except scientific or technical ones. This is because actual requirements about referencing, formats and so on are almost identical. However, it is worth noting one thing about writing up your leadership project or dissertation and this is actually about the words 'leadership' and 'management'. The definitions of these were discussed in Chapter One and the point to be made in writing up your work is that you need to show complete consistency in your use of these words. Be clear that if you have referred to 'leader' on one occasion, this should be retained for the same person, and similarly with 'manager(s)'. As Chapter

One explained, leaders also perform management tasks, in many experts' views, so we are not suggesting complete separation of the terms. In some countries, the terms may be used almost interchangeably, as well as 'administration' which means different things in different countries. With this potential confusion in mind, we are simply asking you to check that you use your own words consistently throughout the writing up of your project.

Summary of Chapter Nine

This chapter has:

- Considered the order in which the project may be written
- Described and discussed the main features of the writing style that is most appropriate for the project
- Raised questions which arise when writing in other than your first language
- Advised on how to avoid plagiarism
- Given clear guidance on the correct use of references and on compiling your Bibliography
- Suggested what is appropriate to include in appendices
- Commented on how to ensure the correct formatting of your work
- Noted the importance of checking your work and suggested ways of doing this
- Given guidelines for writing acknowledgements
- Provided advice, with examples, on writing an abstract.

Further reading

Bailey, S. (2006) *Academic Writing: A Handbook for International Students.* Abingdon: Routledge.

Craswell, G. (2005) *Writing for Academic Success: A Postgraduate Guide.* London: Sage.

10
Understanding Assessment

Introduction

Before you embark on your Masters Level project you will need to have a detailed understanding of the assessment process. This will enable you to structure your completed project to meet particular requirements and give you the best possible chance of success. Each HE institution will have specific assessment guidelines and you need to spend some time familiarising yourself with them. The assessment criteria for your project will be similar but not necessarily the same as the assessment criteria for your other assignments, so make sure you take the time to carefully read the assessment guidance for your project that you have been given in your course documentation. In this chapter we will look in general at assessment strategies and criteria that are employed by HE institutions at Masters Level. We will provide specific examples of how you can meet the assessment requirements and avoid some of the common errors made when writing and submitting your Masters Level project.

In this chapter the following topics are considered:

- Purposes of assessment
- Receiving and acting on feedback
- Understanding the concepts involved in assessment
- Presentation conventions
- Assessment conventions.

Purpose and methods of assessment

As a Masters Level student you may have felt, at times, that there is little purpose to some of the assessment requirements of your particular course.

However, in reality, this should not be the case and you should be aware of the reasons why you are being asked to complete individual assignments. The project provides you with an opportunity to consider an area of interest in greater depth. It should illustrate your ability to analyse and synthesise relevant literature, present arguments supported by relevant evidence and logical discussion and acknowledge sources of ideas and information. Another fundamental requirement for this aspect of your Masters Level degree is that the work is well planned and presented. The project should be the product of your own experience, reading and reflection. Your project will be the culmination of your period of study and should provide you with the opportunity to:

- Write at length on a topic of your choice
- Undertake a review of the available literature
- Consider methodological issues
- Use a variety of data collection methods
- Describe and analyse data
- Develop a number of conclusions and recommendations for policy, your practice and your institution.

The assessment procedure will reflect these requirements and the support process leading up to the final assessment should enable you to meet the requirements. Finding out if you have successfully met the assessment requirements at the end of the programme is necessary, but you also need to know how well you are doing as you proceed through your project. Your HE institution will also want to know how well you have met the requirements of the programme and keep a check on your progress. Basically there are two forms of assessment:

- *Formative assessment*: This method of assessment provides you with 'feed-back' and 'feedforward' as you move through your project. You are then able to take the feedback you have been given and use it in the next phase of your work, 'feedforward', to improve the quality of your work. We will look in more detail about the ways you can make the best use of 'feedback' and 'feedfor-ward' in the next section. Within the life-time of your project your tutor will be providing you with formative assessment to enable you to achieve the best possible outcome for you. The previous work you have completed, as part of your Masters Level programme, can also be used as part of this formative process. You should be taking the feedback from your previous written work into account when working on your project. Formative assessment is basically concerned with finding out how well you are doing and taking action to improve your work as a result of this process.
- *Summative assessment*: This method of assessment also provides you with feedback about what you have done, and it is normally given at the end of a phase of the project or at the very end of the project. Normally summative

assessment is associated with the award of a grade or mark and it usually means you have reached the end of a specific part of your programme. In this book in general, and in this chapter in particular, we are trying to give you the best opportunity to get the highest possible outcome in your summative assessment. You need to aim to complete the project to the highest standard you can achieve. Summative assessment is basically concerned with finding out how well you have done and recording a grade or mark.

Brooks (2007: 115) sums up the difference between the two types of assessment by suggesting you ask yourself: 'Is this assessment FOR learning (formative) or assessment OF learning (summative)?' As you complete your project you will need to make extensive use of formative assessment to maximise your chances of success.

Receiving and acting on feedback

You will receive feedback from a range of people during your Masters Level programme. Your colleagues, friends, research subjects, will, at times, provide you with feedback about what you are doing and the progress you are making. However, as we discussed in Chapter Eight, your tutor will be the person who provides you with the most important feedback. You can expect to receive two forms of feedback from your tutor: oral feedback and written feedback.

Oral feedback

Your tutor should meet you on a regular basis to discuss progress and during the meeting you should take notes to ensure you have a record of the issues that have been discussed. From this record you will be able to develop a series of action points to take your research forward. The meeting with your tutor should be a dialogue and you will be expected to contribute and also to have responded to the tasks previously agreed. Do not be afraid to ask for clarification if you do not understand something that you have discussed with your tutor. Most HE institutions will have an electronic pro forma to record meetings with a tutor – see Figure 10.1.

Written feedback

The written feedback you receive from your tutor for your project should be formative and lead to an improvement in the quality of your work. Whilst useful, written feedback at the end of the project will not enable you to improve

Postgraduate Supervision Record Sheet

Student: *Supervisor:*

FT/PT: **Date:**

Year of study: **Duration:**

Programme: **Supervision focus:**

Ed.D/MPhil/PhD   ☐   *Assignment*   ☐

MA   ☐   *Dissertation*   ☐

Key areas of discussion:

Agreed action points:

Signed: _____ **(Student)**

Signed: _____ **(Supervisor)**

Date of next supervision:

Figure 10.1   An example of a pro forma to record key points of a meeting between student and tutor

the outcome. Therefore, you need to make use of written feedback as you work on your project. If you submit written work as a draft to your tutor you can expect to receive written feedback. You will previously have completed assignments as part of your Masters Level programme and received written feedback. It is worth looking at the feedback you have been given previously and seeing how this can be related to your Masters Level project. We will explore the concepts you are expected to focus on in the next section.

The 'golden rule' here is:

Do not be afraid to ask for clarification from your tutor if you do not understand the oral or written feedback you have been given. Remember, a key role of your tutor is to provide you with clear and consistent feedback about your work.

Understanding the concepts involved in assessment

You will have become accustomed to receiving comments on your written work, often contained in a feedback sheet similar to the one shown in Figure 10.2.

The feedback sheet provides you with detailed information on the particular criteria that are assessed on at Masters Level. You should pay attention to the feedback you have received, and in particular any advice for future work. When you write up your project you need to be aware that you have to meet the criteria that have been given to you. In addition you may also have received specific written guidance about grades and what you need to achieve in order to be awarded a particular mark in your final assessment. We have compiled an example, based on descriptors from a number of HE institutions, of the specific written guidance which describes the various levels you might achieve – see Figure 10.3.

These rather broad guidelines can be further broken down to provide additional advice giving more specific details about the individual marks that are awarded:

- **80%+ An exceptional piece of work**, with total understanding of the subject matter, with a highly developed ability to analyse, synthesise and apply knowledge and concepts. All the objectives of the set work are covered, and there is evidence of critical reflection, originality of thought and creativity. The work is free of errors with a very high level of technical competence. Ideas are fully developed and expressed with fluency in an appropriate manner with an excellent written style.
- **70%–79% An excellent piece of work**, with a good degree of mastery of the subject matter, with a very well developed ability to analyse, synthesise and

Student number: Module: Dissertation/Assignment Title:	Agreed Grade: Percentage:
Overall Comment	
Subject Knowledge	
Analysis and Critique	
Presentation	
Advice for Future Work	
Signed (First Marker):	**Date:**
Second Marker's Comments (where applicable): **Signed (Second Marker):** **Date:**	

Figure 10.2   Feedback sheet

Grade	Subject Knowledge	Analysis and Critique	Presentation
A*/A (Mark of 80% or above = A*; 70%–79% = A)	Displays a highly developed understanding of relevant concepts, theories and/or research methodologies. A wide range of relevant sources, which are well understood, are deployed to support arguments. Excellent subject knowledge.	Recognises the demands of the question, providing a well-focused, relevant answer. Sets sources and viewpoints in a wide context and makes a comprehensive assessment of issues involved. Displays awareness of methodological and theoretical considerations. High levels of ability to analyse, synthesise and apply knowledge and concepts. Detailed examination of issues with reasons for conclusions clearly indicated. Persuasively argued with main issues convincingly evaluated. Evidence of some originality of thought and creativity.	Material is very well-organised and the structure complements the content. A high level of written communication with very few errors of spelling, grammar and syntax. Mastery of referencing conventions with very few errors or omissions. Appropriate length. Followed accepted guidelines for presentation.
B (Mark of 60%—69%)	Sound and thorough grasp of relevant concepts, theories and/or research methodologies although lacking in depth at some points. The work is supported by references to a good range of relevant sources which are used in a relevant way. Good subject knowledge.	Recognises the demands of the question providing a focused, relevant answer which brings out useful points and substantiates them. A good attempt at analysis, synthesis and application of knowledge and concepts. Appreciates main issues and able to make appropriate critical points. Perceptive commentary on evidence and materials used to develop an argument.	Well-structured work displaying attention to the logic and development of the piece. A clear written style. Spelling, grammar and syntax are generally good. Most features of the referencing system are used correctly. Appropriate length.
C (Mark of 50%—59%) Pass Mark 50%	Understanding of main concepts, theories and/or research methodologies is fair but lacks depth and/or breadth. There may be some gaps or areas of confusion. An adequate range of relevant source materials is used. Basic subject knowledge.	Although the demands of the question have been recognised, only the basic requirements are covered and there may be some irrelevant material. The attempt at analysis, synthesis and application of knowledge and concepts is competent but lacks depth and breadth. Sensible commentary on evidence and materials used though some points may be unsubstantiated.	A generally satisfactory overall structure although it may lack balance in parts or fail to integrate some material. An adequate written style which is not impaired by the occasional errors of spelling, grammar and/or syntax. The recommended referencing system is used but with some errors and omissions. Control of length may be less secure, although adequate.

(Continued)

(Continued)

Grade	Subject Knowledge	Analysis and Critique	Presentation
D (Mark of 40%–49%) Fail	Limited evidence of reading but understanding of the subject matter is restricted. The work displays major gaps in knowledge, serious misconceptions and/or factual inaccuracies. Insufficient subject knowledge.	Introduction of basic concepts and effort made to relate them to the demands of the question which have been only partially understood. Mainly descriptive with much irrelevance and unsubstantiated conclusions. No sustained analysis and an inability to apply knowledge and synthesise material. Uncritical exegesis.	Weak structure. Expression of ideas is sometimes confused or unclear. Communication may also be impaired by frequent errors of spelling, grammar and/or syntax. Referencing marred by frequent errors and omissions. May exceed or fail to meet length requirements.
E (Mark below 40%) Fail	Few, if any, relevant source materials used. Serious gaps and/or errors in knowledge and understanding indicate that the student has failed to engage seriously with the subject matter.	The question may have been ignored or badly misunderstood. Few or none of the basic requirements of the project have been achieved. Superficial treatment of the topic much of which is descriptive, irrelevant and unsubstantiated. Lacks appropriate critical or theoretical framework.	Unstructured presentation, lacking coherence. Expression of ideas is poor. Communication may also be impaired by frequent errors of spelling, grammar and/or syntax. The recommended referencing system has not been mastered. Length requirements not met.

Figure 10.3 Specific written guidance describing the various levels that can be achieved

apply knowledge and concepts. All the major objectives of the set work are covered, and there is evidence of critical reflection. The work is free of all but very minor errors, with a high level of technical competence. Ideas are expressed with fluency with a very good written style.

- **60%–69% A good piece of work**, displaying a sound and thorough grasp of the subject matter, though lacking in the breadth and depth required for a first-class mark. There is a good attempt at analysis, synthesis and application of knowledge and concepts, but the work is more limited in scope than that required for the higher mark. Most objectives of the work set are covered and there is some evidence of critical reflection. The work is generally technically competent. Ideas are expressed clearly, with minor exceptions.
- **50%–59% An adequate piece of work**, showing a grasp of major components of the subject matter but possibly with some gaps or areas of confusion. Only the basic requirements of the work set are covered. The attempt at analysis, synthesis and application of knowledge and concepts is superficial and limited. There is a heavy reliance on basic course materials. The work may contain some errors, and technical competence is at a routine level only. There is little critical reflection and there is some confusion in expression of ideas with a restricted written style.

Any mark below 50 is a fail and if you are awarded below this figure you will have failed your project and your Masters Degree. As a minimum you need to aim to get beyond this level and hopefully closer to the 80% mark than the bare minimum!

- **40%–49% Fail, not of a passable level for a postgraduate programme**. This is a poor piece of work, showing some familiarity with the subject matter, but with major gaps and serious misconceptions that are obvious to the examiner. Only some of the basic requirements of the work set are achieved by the student. There is little or no attempt at analysis, synthesis or application of knowledge, and a low level of technical competence, with many basic errors. There is an inability to reflect critically on an argument or viewpoint. The ideas are poorly developed, expressed and structured with a poor written style.
- **Below 40% Absolute fail, work not of passable standard**. There are serious gaps in knowledge and understanding of the subject matter, and many areas of confusion. Few or none of the basic requirements of the work set are achieved, and there is an inability to apply knowledge. Technical competence is poor, with many serious errors. The level of expression and structure is very inadequate with many errors in presentation. The student has failed to engage deeply or seriously with any of the subject matter involved.

This information is extremely useful and provides you with guidance about what you need to do to reach a particular level. It is worth spending some time going through each of the descriptors and identifying key words and phrases that you want to focus on. If we take the 80%+ descriptor we would identify as significant: *analyse; synthesise; originality of thought; apply knowledge and concepts; critical reflection; creativity; ideas are fully developed.*

Let us compare these positive comments to the words and phrases contained in the 40%–49% fail descriptor: *major gaps and serious misconceptions; basic errors; no attempt at analysis, synthesis or application; inability to reflect critically; low level of technical competence.*

You can see the obvious differences between the two descriptors, and you need to use this information to make sure you aim to reach the highest level possible. Thinking about what you need to be successful in your Masters Level project is not sufficient in itself to guarantee success, but it is a legitimate starting point. Make sure you are fully aware of what is required of you as a student and aim to reach that standard. Having identified some key words and phrases we now need to consider what these words and phrases actually mean to you as a student attempting to successfully complete your Masters Level project. Let us now consider some of the individual assessment areas that are identified in the above examples in more detail.

Subject knowledge

Your examiner will expect you to have a detailed subject knowledge of the area you are investigating. You are investigating an area of your choice, in depth, and you will come to know the area in great detail, perhaps even more so than your tutor does. You need to display this knowledge and prove that you have developed detailed subject knowledge by making sure you carry out a thorough literature review of the area (see Chapter Three). You have to look at a wide range of source material and this will involve an extensive literature search. However, at this level, it is not sufficient to list the various sources you have looked at as part of your project. You will need to properly interrogate the literature and show that you understand the area. The source material you have accessed can then be used to support the arguments you develop. We have looked at this aspect in detail in Chapter Three and you must be sure that you understand the need to undertake critical analysis of the source material you have used. Making sure you read materials properly will lead to quality writing and enable you to show that you have good subject knowledge.

Analysis

Many Masters Level students receive this type of feedback on their written work from their tutor:

You need to develop the skills of analysis and to move beyond description. In particular you need to focus on considering a wide range of issues and developing a coherent examination of knowledge and concepts. Analysis is by far the most important skill you need to develop at this level. Description, whilst necessary, will not enable you to reach the required standard at this level. You need to work on developing improved analysis and reflection and displaying these skills in your written work.

So, what does this type of comment from a tutor actually mean and just what does a tutor mean when asking you to develop the 'skills of analysis'? During their Masters Level programme many students find analysis the area they have most difficulty with. Analysis requires you to break a topic down into its various sections and interrogate the nature of the sections and their connection with each other. In particular, you are required to display your arguments in a wide context and to develop a coherent argument. You do this by examining the issue fully, not just putting forward one point of view. You need to develop the capacity to think and reflect about the concepts you are using and explain your thinking and reflection to the person reading your work.

Description

In the tutor feedback in the previous section, description is described as 'necessary'. You clearly need to describe events or the situation you are looking at, but you have to go beyond mere description. As a starting point you have to provide a detailed account and then build on the description you have provided. Let us give an example of how you take your basic description and move beyond this starting point.

Within your project you will have carried out some form of research and you will need to describe the methodology you have used. You would describe how you carried out, for example, your semi-structured interviews, and the methods you used to develop and distribute the questionnaires you administered. You will need to describe your methodology to enable the person reading your project to understand what you have done. However, you need to move beyond this and to analyse the methodology by examining the methods you have used and by explaining why you selected a particular approach. You would undertake this analysis by considering the advantages and disadvantages of the methods you have employed, by discussing how they could have been improved and by suggesting alterations and improvements. In addition you could consider alternative data collection methods and finally support your arguments by drawing on some of the available research methodology literature to show you have developed a detailed understanding of the topic.

Critique

When asked to undertake a critique of theories or assertions students often think they have to be critical or negative about the topic. Whilst you are being asked to question or interrogate a particular topic it does not automatically follow that the outcome has to be critical. You need to develop a questioning approach to your work and not to accept policy, ideas or claims at face value. A critical approach should always be applied to all aspects of your work. Do not be afraid to question official policies and publications and published work from established academics. Of course your critique has to be based on sound arguments and draw on evidence from your own research and from your reading. A critique cannot be justified on the grounds that you just do not like a particular policy or idea. By all means question and disagree with current ideas and policies but do not allow your own prejudices to cloud your judgement.

The 'golden rule' is:

Always support your own opinions with evidence from the literature or from your own research.

Evaluate

An important part of your project will involve the collection of a range of evidence from a variety of sources. You will need to make some decisions based on the evidence you have collected and provide a justification for the judgements you have reached. Evaluation is related to analysis and critique, but it also requires you to come to some form of conclusion about the evidence you have presented. If you think of the task of a jury in a court you will be able to understand the process of evaluation. You are expected to take the evidence and to reach a decision or conclusion based on the evidence you have received. In the case of your research you will be reaching conclusions on a particular aspect of policy or of a certain initiative and deciding how effective it has been. The evidence you select will be important and you need to make sure it is, wherever possible, recent and of course relevant.

Presentation conventions

Your Masters Level project will allow you to demonstrate that you have a thorough and detailed understanding of a topic of your choice and that you have carried out an original piece of research. You will be expected to present your final piece of work in a particular format that conforms to the format which we introduced in the previous chapter. You will be required to focus on four specific aspects of presentation:

- Structure and writing style
- Presentation of data
- Referencing
- Technical requirements.

Structure and writing style

By the time you come to write up your Masters Level project you will already have developed your own writing style. Provided your style has been acceptable and successful you should not attempt to do anything different for your project. The basic requirements of clarity and structure will apply to any piece of written work and of course the necessity to answer the question is paramount. Clarity of communication and clear presentation of data is important to enable you to show the examiner that you know your subject area. As we explained in Chapter Two you would normally expect to find the following chapters in the main text of a Masters Level project:

- Introduction
- Literature review
- Methodology
- Research findings
- Analysis of findings
- Conclusion and recommendations
- References
- Appendices.

Presentation of data

You will only have a limited number of words for your project and you may have accumulated a large amount of data. You do not have to show all your original data, but you have to present the data in an acceptable format. For example, illustrations of original data, questionnaires and interview schedules, can be included in appendices, but the data you have collected has to be included in your findings chapter. Quotes from interviews can be used to support key points or to help the development of a case study approach, but you would not include full transcripts of all the interviews you have completed. The use of diagrams and charts will make the presentation of data much easier and more accessible for the examiner. You need to think very carefully about the best methods to use to present your findings to maximise the impact of the data. For further details on the presentation of data, see Chapter Seven.

Referencing

Again this is an area that often causes problems for students. The best advice is to follow the conventions laid down by your own HE institution. You will have been given clear written guidance in your course handbook and you must follow the guidelines as laid down and those which we outlined in Chapter Nine.

Technical Requirements

Each HE institution will have particular technical requirements that you have to conform to and you will be provided with details of these. Below is an example of the type of guidance you may receive:

(A) *Presentation of the Dissertation / Extended Project*
     Projects should be typewritten on A4 good quality paper, double spaced, with a margin of at least 4cm on the left hand side. Adequate margins should also be left on the other three edges. Page numbers should be included. You should carefully proof-read your work for typographical errors and correct them before submitting the dissertation. Please use 12 point Arial or Times New Roman font.

(B) *Binding*
     You are required to submit two copies of the project in soft binding (red) to Reception in the Department by **1st September**. The Print Office (on central campus) can provide this form of binding cheaply. You should paste a white label on the front of each copy with your name, the title, the title of the degree you are registered for (e.g. MA in Educational Leadership and Innovation) and the name of the Department responsible.

(C) *Title*
     The title should describe the content of the tendered project accurately and concisely and will have been previously agreed with your tutor.

(D) *Title Page*
     The title page should give the following information in the order listed:

     • Full title of the dissertation/extended project and subtitle if any
     • Full name, followed, if so desired, by any qualifications

- Statement: 'Dissertation/extended project presented as a partial requirement for the award of ...'
- Affiliation
- Date: month and year of submission.

(E) *Table of Contents*
This should immediately follow the title page. It should list in sequence, with page numbers, all relevant subdivisions of the dissertation/ extended project.

(F) *Acknowledgements*
This is normally on the page following the table of contents and you will acknowledge people who have provided you with support.

(G) *Abstract*
You must provide a summary of the work not exceeding 300 words (a single page). Single spaced typing is permitted. This should be a synopsis of the work and provide an indication of its nature and scope. A brief statement of the method of investigation together with the main argument and conclusion should be included, but it has to be brief.

(H) *Ethics*
You should ensure that you comply with all the elements specified on the ethical approval form; for example, making participants and organisations anonymous.

(I) *Appendices*
You should include a copy of your signed ethical approval form as an appendix. You may wish to include a copy of your research instrument or some examples of transcript data as other appendices. Resist the temptation to use your appendices as a means of getting around the word limit.

The technical requirements are a necessary and important part of the assessment process and if you do not follow the guidelines your project will not be accepted for marking and you will be required to resubmit your project. The technical requirements might seem relatively minor given the amount of work you have done, but they are crucial to the successful outcome of your project.

Assessment conventions

Again each HE institution will have their own assessment conventions and you need to familiarise yourself with those that are relevant to you. We include some examples of the type of assessment conventions found in most HE institutions.

Feedback on assessed work (projects)

Your Masters Level work which counts towards your final qualification is assessed holistically. This means that the mark awarded is based on an overall judgement of the quality of the work against relevant assessment criteria. We have looked at examples of these criteria earlier in the chapter. Individual assessment criteria are not normally separately assessed nor are they allocated a separate mark weighting. The feedback you receive will take the form of written comments plus a letter grade and a percentage based on the following mark scheme.

All written work that counts towards your qualification is considered by more than one marker. In most HE institutions all projects will be second marked, but on many programmes only those on a grade borderline or with a fail mark are subject to double marking. On the rare occasions where agreement on the grading of an assignment cannot be reached by the first marker and moderator/second marker, the course leader will nominate a third marker. If the disagreement is not resolved in this way, the work will be referred to the Director of Postgraduate Taught Courses who will review the marking and make a final decision. External examiners act in a moderating role, receiving samples of marked projects. External examiners are experts in the area from another institution and you may get the opportunity to meet them as part of the review of your programme. In most cases marks and grades are provisional until they have been formally agreed by the University Examination Board. As a general rule, you should expect your work to be marked and returned about a month after the submission date, although formal ratification by the Examination Board might take longer and will depend on the conventions in your HE institution.

Board of Examiners (Examination Board)

All programmes will have a Board of Examiners which takes the final decision about the marks and grades awarded to each candidate. The Board of Examiners is made up of staff from your institution who work on your programme and the external examiners for the programme and will discuss the progress of every candidate. It will consider all mark/grade recommendations and it then passes its recommendations to the University Senate for final approval. The Examination Board may recommend that a candidate who has failed components of a course (written assignments/project) should be allowed to resubmit the failed components within a time limit prescribed by the Board. You will normally have the right of appeal against any decision taken by the Board of Examiners provided you have reasonable grounds on which to appeal. If you are in this unfortunate position you will need to consult your own HE institution regulations which will set out any grounds for appeal.

Cheating and plagiarism

Cheating and plagiarism is defined as an attempt to benefit oneself, or someone else, by deceit or fraud. These are serious offences which will adversely affect your final result if proven. They should be avoided at all costs and we have written about the strategies you have to follow to avoid plagiarism in Chapter Nine.

When you submit your project you will have to complete a declaration that you have read and understood the guidance on plagiarism that has been provided to you, and that the project represents your own work and includes appropriate acknowledgements to the work of others. Heavy reliance on acknowledged sources does not constitute plagiarism but may be considered poor scholarship and your project may be marked down accordingly, especially if the range of sources you have used is limited. Many institutions have an electronic checking system for plagiarism and written work is routinely submitted for plagiarism checking.

You should not under any circumstances use web-based, or hard copy posted projects from project banks for your assessed or unassessed work. Quite apart from the fact that the vast majority of such material is badly written and of poor analytical quality, this is direct cheating. If you are discovered to have been using such material, you are liable to fail and also to be disciplined for cheating, with potentially very severe penalties.

In practice, few students are deliberately dishonest and many cases of plagiarism arise from bad scholarly practice or a misunderstanding of the accepted conventions. There is nothing wrong with using other people's ideas. Indeed, citing other people's work shows that you have researched your topic and have used their thinking to help formulate your own argument. Such an intelligent survey and synthesis of existing views might, indeed, form the basis of your work. The important thing is to know what is yours and what is not, and to communicate this clearly to the person who is examining your work.

The 'golden rule' is:

Make sure you follow the referencing conventions properly and that all quotations from sources are acknowledged every time they occur in your work.

Summary of Chapter Ten

This chapter has:

- Identified the purposes of assessment
- Discussed the process of feedback
- Provided a greater understanding of assessment concepts
- Explored presentation and assessment conventions.

Further reading

The official and up-to-date handbook of your own HE institution (Graduate Studies or Dissertation/Project Handbook).

Boud, D. and Falchikov, N. (2007) *Rethinking Assessment in Higher Education*. London: Routledge.

11

Next Steps

It is unlikely that you have read a book such as this from cover to cover, finally arriving at this chapter. It is more likely that you will have looked at the contents list of chapter titles and topics, picked out those which you need most help with and read those first. However, whatever your personal approach, we would like in this final brief chapter to:

- Remind you of our 'golden rules'
- Select some of the most important issues for your attention
- Suggest how to actually get started – and finally –
- Suggest some practical things that you might do next, as you begin your journey.

Some golden rules

Throughout the book, we have identified in each chapter at least one – and sometimes more than one – thing which is in our view essential to success in a particular area of your project work. We have called these our 'golden rules'. Mostly, we have given advice or guidelines as to what you should do, but these action points are so important that we believe we can say these MUST be done for success to be achieved. Let us remind you of them (we have combined some and modified others to make them easier to remember):

1. Context of your study – ENSURE THE CONTEXT IS REALISTIC AND MANAGEABLE BEFORE YOU EMBARK ON THE PROJECT.
2. Choice of topic – CHOOSE A TOPIC IN WHICH YOU HAVE A GENUINE INTEREST AND IN WHICH YOU CAN DEVELOP THE SKILLS YOU HAVE.

3. Literature review – ENSURE YOU DEVELOP A CRITICAL APPROACH IN WRITING YOUR REVIEW OF THE LITERATURE.
4. Research methods – ENSURE YOU KNOW WHICH DATA YOU NEED TO COLLECT BEFORE DECIDING UPON THE METHOD OF COLLECTING THE DATA.
5. Sampling – IN SAMPLING, DECIDE FIRST ON WHICH PEOPLE AND THEN ON HOW MANY.
6. Ethics in research – REMEMBER NEVER TO TAKE ACCESS TO OR THE CO-OPERATION OF PARTICIPANTS FOR GRANTED. KEEP PEOPLE INFORMED OF YOUR PROGRESS AND MAINTAIN AN OPEN DIALOGUE WITH ALL PARTICIPANTS.
7. Presenting findings – ENSURE YOU KEEP THE PRESENTATION OF YOUR FINDINGS DATA SEPARATE FROM YOUR ANALYSIS OF THAT DATA.
8. Analysis – PLAY TO YOUR PERSONAL STRENGTHS IN CARRYING OUT YOUR ANALYSIS BY USING THE SKILLS YOU HAVE DEVELOPED AND IN WHICH YOU HAVE MOST CONFIDENCE.
9. Conclusions – ALWAYS SUPPORT YOUR OPINIONS WITH EVIDENCE FROM THE LITERATURE AND/OR FROM YOUR OWN RESEARCH.
10. Avoiding plagiarism – TO AVOID UNINTENTIONAL PLAGIARISM, KEEP A CAREFUL RECORD OF THE SOURCES OF EVERYTHING YOU USE.
11. Using support – DO NOT BE AFRAID TO ASK FOR CLARIFICATION FROM YOUR TUTOR IF YOU DO NOT UNDERSTAND THE ORAL OR WRITTEN FEEDBACK YOU HAVE BEEN GIVEN.
12. Understanding assessment – ENSURE YOU KNOW THE CRITERIA WHICH WILL BE USED IN ASSESSING YOUR WORK IN THE INSTITUTION WHERE YOU ARE REGISTERED.

Important issues

The two biggest issues that you have to face at the start are:

- WHAT is going to be the topic for this project?
- HOW am I going to research it?

We have given detailed advice about these issues in Chapters One and Two, but at this early stage, you may flounder a little. So, listen to advice from:

- Friends
- Work peer colleagues
- Work managers or leaders
- Sponsors
- Academic staff, especially your tutor/supervisor.

But it is YOUR decision – you are the one doing the research and writing the final piece of work, not them! Thus we suggest Golden Rules 1 and 2 (above) override everything else at the moment.

As well as potential helpers and advisers, it is a good idea to identify any potential barriers or hindrances to what you are aiming for. These could include:

- Personal circumstances, now and in the period ahead
- Work demands
- People who may not be as co-operative as you need them to be to do your project effectively
- Shortage of time
- Access to resources.

You could use an adaptation of a 'force field analysis' to set out the pros and cons for any potential topic and methodologies. On a sheet of paper, draw a line down the middle and list on one side of the line those things (or 'forces') which seem to be likely to help you succeed and on the other those 'forces' which may be working against its success. This is a subjective exercise so you can do it privately and it can help to clarify your thinking. For example, a colleague who you feel rather resents your being sponsored for the course and may not be very helpful would be on the 'cons' side, whereas the fact that you have access to a large personal library of books on leadership would obviously be a 'pro'. See Figure 11.1 for an example. When all are listed, try to 'weigh' them. Which are major? Which are trivial? Can you prioritise the pros and cons? Again, we stress it is YOUR decision.

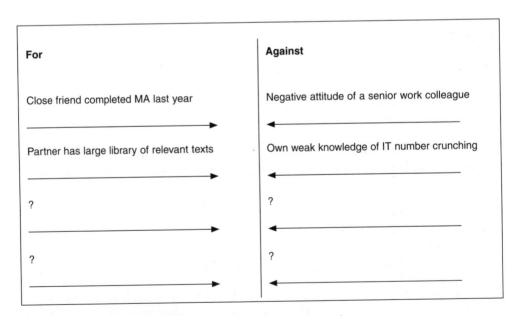

Figure 11.1   A force field analysis of possible choices in research

Getting started

For most Masters Level students the most difficult part of the whole thing is actually just this – getting started! Do you remember your very first written assignment that you had to do? Do you recall how you felt at that time? For some students, that was the first piece of written work that they had had to do since being at University or College a number of years ago. Even for experienced teachers, for example, who have regularly written handbooks, policies, syllabuses, starting their first assignment of this kind was daunting as it is a very different kind of writing. If you are fresh from a first degree course, you will certainly be used to writing essays, but you have to note that Masters Level work is NOT the same as first degree work and you need to adjust accordingly.

Here are some of the things you might consider doing to get yourself started:

- Read back through your previous assignments on the programme. Note the comments from the assessors. Some will be from your tutor but some may be from second markers or moderators. Did the comments on the most recent assignments reveal anything about your development? If so, in which areas? Did they show you had acted upon advice given?
- Identify the skills areas where you think you have been most successful, perhaps where you have developed most. Are there areas which you still find particularly difficult or problematic? Should these be ones which you would be wise to avoid in your final and most demanding piece of work? Are you primarily a quantitative person or a qualitative one (see Chapter Two), for example?
- Ask yourself what you actually ENJOY doing in this kind of work. Do you enjoy interviewing other people? Do you like designing questionnaires? Do you like reading and analysing documents?
- Make sure you are clear in your own mind what you understand by 'leadership and 'management' (see Chapter One), whatever others say. As long as you back your view from reading or research, your opinion counts!
- Scan the adverts and noticeboards to see if any conferences/short courses are due in the near future and if they are affordable. Is there something on leadership or on research methods coming up that could be useful? If you cannot go, perhaps someone else from your place of work is attending – make sure you get all the notes and handouts from them. It does not matter if you disagree with all that is presented at a conference – it all helps the debate! Choose carefully in terms of timing. A seminar on, for example, 'A Whole New Approach to Leadership: Changing your Mindset' could be inspiring or provocative as you begin, but could be confidence sapping halfway through your project if it unsettles all your thinking on which you have been basing your work!
- READ! If you are not a member of a library, join now. If you are, make sure you renew your membership/subscription to cover the period of your project. Check

whether your own institution already subscribes to and receives journals from various practitioner/leadership/management organisations. It is our experience that many workplaces receive them but they are only circulated to a limited readership – they can get 'stuck' in managers' offices! Remind whomever it is that you are now doing a Masters in X or Y and you would be grateful to be on the circulation list. Most organisations are only too pleased that others in the workplace want to read the journals. A possible bonus outcome is that when you have successfully completed your Masters, you may want to contact one of these journals about publishing some of your work – they are usually keen to hear from practitioners in this respect.

- Start saving articles NOW from good quality journals, magazines and features in 'quality' newspapers. You may never use many of them but it will be worth it if just a few are useful. Some have the author's contact (email) at the end of a populist article where full details of a research project can be located and downloaded.
- See if there are any seminars in the offing in your own HE institution about leadership and management, or about research methods. Visiting speakers such as management 'gurus' or Professors of Leadership often give lectures and you will usually be welcome to boost the numbers. Do not be afraid at the end of a very good public lecture to approach the speaker, tell them you are studying that topic and ask if you could contact them if the need arose. Such speakers often welcome such interest being shown, and will sometimes send material to you.

As mentioned above, discuss with your tutor, colleagues, friends, previous graduates, ideas you may have. Look at previous projects or dissertations as well. These are normally held in your institution's library.

What to do now!

We suggest:

- Decide on the filing system you are going to use and stick to it. Whether it is box files of sundry pieces of paper or spreadsheets of data of various kinds, or a mixture of both – whichever works for you – make your mind up on this and enter everything in a logical way into YOUR system. There is no single right way – just the right way for YOU. However, make sure you keep accurate and accessible records of everything you read.
- Draw up an outline of a personal timetable for the period ahead, covering up to when you plan to complete the project. This will almost certainly be altered, perhaps drastically, but you need to have a calendar at this stage. It might cover, for example:

BY AUGUST 31 – Decide on topic.

BY SEPTEMBER 24 – Meet tutor, confirm topic and outline of methodology.

BY OCTOBER 10 – Submit official proposal to office – methodology confirmed. Submit ethical approval form.

BY OCTOBER 31 – All letters to firms/organisations written. Questionnaires constructed and out for piloting.

Context and Purpose written and sent to tutor.

BY MID NOVEMBER – Replies to letters received – chase up non-replies. Amend questionnaires after piloting. Telephone re interviews – try to arrange for late November/early December.

EARLY DECEMBER – Do interviews. Arrange observations for January.

BY JANUARY 31 – Complete Literature Review draft – submit to tutor.

BY END MARCH – All field work completed!

BY END APRIL – Set out data.

BY END MAY – Complete analysis!

BY END JUNE – Begin writing up sections on Methodology and on Findings.

BY END JULY – Write Conclusions, etc.

BY END AUGUST – Complete – and submit!!!

Note the dates are looser as the year proceeds. This is because things do not always go according to plan. We would advise including fixed dates when you will do nothing on the project, such as 'Away for Xmas December 22–29' or 'Family visiting May 26–30'. If you do something then, it is a bonus but prepare to write off certain dates. As we have said, any timetable will be altered significantly as soon as things really get underway but make sure you have an outline to start with.

- Finally, as soon as possible, MAKE A START! Do not be afraid to take the plunge and write the first two or three hundred words describing the context in which you operate. Where do you work? What are some of the details of the place? Is it typical of its kind? How long have you worked there? What do you do? This is a very easy piece of writing to do. Any professional writer will tell you that doing this 'plunging in' is essential. It does not matter that later on you may completely rewrite this piece – what you will gain is confidence in the process of writing and the feeling that you have actually started. No one else has to read this, unless you wish them to do so! The feeling of satisfaction at having started by having written a couple of hundred words is something that many of our own students have told us about – and something we have experienced ourselves.

So, get started and we hope that you will find yourself looking back through various parts of this book when you need help. Good luck – we wish you every success with your personal project or dissertation in some area of leadership or management and hope that this book will have helped you in some measure to achieve your Masters Degree.

Glossary of Terms Used

BIS	Business, Innovation and Skills
CRB	Criminal Records Bureau
DfE	Department for Education
Ed.D.	Doctor of Education
FT	Full-time
GCSE	General Certificate of Secondary Education
HE	Higher Education
HOD	Head of Department
HOY	Head of Year
HRM	Human Resource Management
ID	Identity
IT	Information Technology
LA	Local Authority
MA	Master of Arts
MBA	Master of Business Administration
M.Phil.	Master of Philosophy
NCSL	National College for School Leadership and Children's Services
Ofsted	Office for Standards in Education
PE	Physical Education
PGCE	Postgraduate Certificate in Education
Ph.D.	Doctor of Philosophy
PT	Part-time
QAS	Quality Assurance Service
SBM	School Based Management/Site Based Management
SIT	School Improvement Team
SWOT	Strengths, Weaknesses, Opportunities, Threats
UK	United Kingdom

References

Adelman, C., Jenkins, D. and Kemmis, S. (1984) 'Rethinking Case Study', in Bell, J., Bush, T., Fox, A., Goodey, J. and Goulding, S. (eds) *Conducting Small-scale Investigations in Educational Management*. London: Harper and Row.

Altrichter, H., Feldman, A., Posch, P. and Somekh, B. (2008) *Teachers Investigate their Work*. London: Routledge.

Bailey, S. (2006) *Academic Writing: A Handbook for International Students*. Abingdon: Routledge.

Bassey, M. (1999) *Case Study Research in Educational Settings*. Buckingham: Open University Press.

Bassey, M. (2002) 'Case Study Research', in Coleman, M. and Briggs, A. (eds) *Research Methods in Educational Management*. London: Sage.

Belbin, M. (1981) *Management Teams: Why they Succeed or Fail*. London: Heinemann.

Bell, J. (2002) 'Questionnaires', in Coleman, M. and Briggs, A. (eds) *Research Methods in Educational Leadership and Management*. London: Sage.

BIS (2010) 'Want to Know More About your Rights at Work? You Have a Powerful Friend', Department for Business, Innovation and Skills.

Black, T. (1999) *Doing Quantitative Research*. London: Sage.

Boud, D. and Falchicov, N. (2007) *Rethinking Assessment in Higher Education*. London: Routledge.

Briggs, A. (2002) 'Academic Writing: Process and Presentation', in Coleman, M. and Briggs, A. (eds) *Research Methods in Educational Leadership and Management*. London: Sage.

Brooks, V. (2007) 'Using assessment for formative purposes', in Brooks, V., Abbott, I. and Bills, L. (eds) *Preparing to Teach in Secondary Schools*. Maidenhead: McGraw Hill.

Burnes, B. (2009) *Managing Change*. London: Prentice Hall.

Bush, T. (2002) 'Authenticity – Reliability, Validity and Triangulation', in Coleman, M. and Briggs, A. (eds) *Research Methods in Educational Leadership and Management*. London: Sage.

Bush, T. and Middlewood, D. (2005) *Leading and Managing People in Education*. London: Sage.

Bush, T., Bell, L. and Middlewood, D. (eds) (2010) *Principles of Educational Leadership and Management*. London: Sage.

Bush, T., Qiang, H. and Fang, J. (1998) 'Educational Management in China: An Overview', *Compare*, 28(2): 133–40.

Busher, H. (2002) 'Ethics of Research in Education', in Coleman, M. and Briggs, A. (eds) *Research Methods in Educational Leadership and Management*. London: Sage.

Campbell, A. and Groundwater-Smith, S. (eds) (2007) *An Ethical Approach to Practitioner Research: Dealing with Issues and Dilemmas in Action Research*. London: Routledge.

Coghlan, D. and Brannick, T. (2009) *Doing Action Research in Your Organization*. London: Sage.

Cohen, L. and Manion, L. (2000) *Research Methods in Education*, 5th edn. London: Routledge.

Coleman, M. and Briggs, A. (2002) *Research Methods in Educational Leadership and Management*. London: Sage.

Cortazzi, M. (2002) 'Analysing Narratives and Documents', in Coleman, M. and Briggs, A. (eds) *Research Methods in Educational Leadership and Management*. London: Sage.

Craswell, G. (2005) *Writing for Academic Success: A Postgraduate Guide*. London: Sage.

Creswell, J. (2002) *Research Design: Qualitative, Quantitative and Mixed Methods Approaches*, 2nd edn. Thousand Oaks, CA: Sage.

Crotty, M. (1998) *The Foundation of Social Research: Meaning and Perspectives in the Research Process*. London: Sage.

Cuban, L. (1988) *The Managerial Imperative and the Practice of Leadership in Schools*. New York: State University of New York Press.

De Laine, M. (2000) *Fieldwork, Participation and Practice: Ethics and Dilemmas in Qualitative Research*. London: Sage.

Denscombe, M. (1998) *The Good Research Guide*. Buckingham: Open University Press.

Denscombe, M. (2002) *Ground Rules for Good Research*. Buckingham: Open University Press.

Denzin, N. and Lincoln, Y. (2000) *Handbook of Qualitative Research*. Thousand Oaks, CA: Sage.

Dimmock, C. (2002) 'Cross-cultural Differences in Interpreting and Doing Research', in Coleman, M. and Briggs, A. (eds) *Research Methods in Educational Leadership and Management*. London: Sage.

Easterby-Smith, M., Thorpe, R. and Lowe, A. (2002) *Management Research: An Introduction*, 2nd edn. London: Sage.

Elliot, J. (1984) 'Improving the Quality of Teaching through Action Research', Forum, 26: 74–7.

Fogelman, K. (2002) 'Surveys and Sampling', in Coleman, M. and Briggs, A. (eds) *Research Methods in Educational Leadership and Management*. London: Sage.

Flowerdew, J. (1999) 'Problems in Writing for Scholarly Publications in English: The Case of Hong Kong', *Journal of Second Language Writing*, 8: 243–64.

Fowler, F. (2002) *Survey Research Methods*. Thousand Oaks, CA: Sage.

Giddings, L. (2006) 'Mixed Methods Research: Positivism Dressed as Drag?', *Journal of Research in Nursing*, 11(3): 195–203.

Glatter, R. (2002) 'Governance, Autonomy and Accountability in Education', in Bush, T. and Bell, L. (eds) *Principles and Practice of Educational Management*. London: Sage.

Gray, D. (2009) *Doing Research in the Real World*, 2nd edn. London: Sage.

Herr, K. and Anderson, G. (2005) *The Action Research Dissertation*. Thousand Oaks, CA: Sage.

Hyland, K. (2004) 'Graduates' Gratitude: The Generic Structure of Dissertation Acknowledgements', *English for Specific Purposes*, 23: 303–24.

James, E.A., Milenkiewicz, M.T. and Bucknam, A. (2008) *Participatory Action Research for Educational Leadership*. Thousand Oaks, CA: Sage.

Jankowicz, A. (2004) *Business Research Projects for Students*, 4th edn. London: Cengage Learning.

Johnson, D. (1994) *Research Methods in Educational Management*. Harlow: Longman.

Koshy, V. (2009) *Action Research for Improving Educational Practice*. London: Sage.

Lewis, J. and Ritchie, J. (2003) 'Generalising from Qualitative Research', in Lewis, J. and Ritchie, J. (eds) *Qualitative Research Practice*. Thousand Oaks, CA: Sage.

Lichtman, M. (2009) *Qualitative Research in Education: A User's Guide*. London: Sage.

Lincoln, Y. and Guba, E. (2000) The Only Generalisation Is: There Is No Generalisation', in Gomm, R., Hammersley, M. and Foster, P. (eds) *Case Study Method: Key Issues, Key Texts*. London: Sage.

McNiff, J. and Whitehead, J. (2005) *All You Need to Know about Action Research*. London: Sage.

McNiff, J. and Whitehead, J. (2009a) *You and Your Action Research Project*. London: Routledge.

McNiff, J. and Whitehead, J. (2009b) *Doing and Writing Action Research*. London: Sage.

Menter, I., Elliott, D., Hall, J., Hall, S., Hulme, M., Lewin, J. and Lowden, K. (2010) *A Guide to Practitioner Research in Education*. London: Sage.

Middlewood, D. (2001) 'The Future of Teacher Performance and its Appraisal', in Middlewood, D. and Cardno, C. (eds) *Managing Teacher Appraisal and Performance: A Comparative Approach*. London: RoutledgeFalmer.

Middlewood, D. (2010) 'Managing People and Performance', in Bush, T., Bell, L. and Middlewood, D. (eds) *Principles of Educational Leadership and Management*. London: Sage.

Middlewood, D., Coleman, M. and Lumby, J. (1999) *Practitioner Research in Education*. London: Paul Chapman Publishing.

Morrison, M. (2002) 'Using Diaries in Research', in Coleman, M. and Briggs, A. (eds) *Research Methods in Educational Leadership and Management*. London: Sage.

Nahavandi, A. (2000) *The Art and Science of Leadership*. Upper Saddle River, NJ: Prentice Hall.

Nisbett, J. and Watt, J. (1984) 'Case Study', in Bell, J., Bush, T., Fox, A., Goodey, J. and Goulding, S. (eds) *Conducting Small-scale Investigations in Educational Management*. London: Harper and Row.

Ofsted (2009) 'Who We Are and What We Do', London: Office for Standards in Education.

Partridge, B. and Starfield, S. (2007) *Thesis and Dissertation Writing in a Second Language*. London: Routledge.

Pell, A. and Fogelman, K. (2002) 'Analysing Quantitative Data', in Coleman, M. and Briggs, A. (eds) *Research Methods in Educational Leadership and Management*. London: Sage.

Popper, K. (1968) *The Logic of Scientific Discovery*, 2nd edn. London: Hutchinson.

Potter, S. (2006) *Doing Postgraduate Research*. London: Sage.

Reason, P. and Bradbury, H. (2007) *The Sage Handbook of Action Research*. London: Sage.

Ridley, D. (2008) *The Literature Review: A Step-by-Step Guide for Students*. London: Sage.

Rumsey, S. (2008) *How to Find Information: A Guide for Researchers*. London: Open University Press.

Sagor, R. (2000) *Guiding School Improvement through Action Research*. Alexandria, VA: Association for Supervision and Curriculum Development.

Scott, J. (1996) *A Matter of Record*. Cambridge: Polity Press.

Somekh, B. (2006) *Action Research: A Methodology for Change and Development*. London: Open University Press.

Southworth, G. (1993) 'School Leadership and School Development', *School Organisation*, 12(2): 73–87.

Theisen, G. and Adams, D. (1990) 'Comparative Education Research', in Thomas, R. (ed.) *International Comparative Education*. Oxford: Pergamon Press.

Watling, R. (2002) 'The Analysis of Qualitative Data', in Coleman, M. and Briggs, A. (eds) *Research Methods in Educational Leadership and Management*. London: Sage.

Wellington, J. (2010) *Making Supervision Work for You: A Student's Guide*. London: Sage.

Williams, G. (1994) 'Observing and Recording Meetings', in Bennett, N., Glatter, R. and Levacic, R. (eds) *Improving Educational Management through Research and Consultancy*. London: Paul Chapman Publishing.

Wragg, E. (2002) 'Interviewing', in Coleman, M. and Briggs, A. (eds) *Research Methods in Educational Leadership and Management*. London: Sage.

Yin, R. (2003) *Case Study Research: Design and Methods*, 3rd edn. Thousand Oaks, CA: Sage.

Yukl, G. (2002) *Leadership in Organisations*. London: Prentice Hall.

Zerubavel, E. (1999) *The Clockwork Muse: A Practical Guide to Writing Theses, Dissertations and Books*. Cambridge, MA: Harvard University Press.

Author Index

Subject Index